Instant Vortex Plus Dual Air Fryer Cookbook For Beginners

1800 Days Instant Vortex Plus Double Decker Air Fryer Recipes Can provide easy to understand instructions and creative ideas

Joyce A. King

Copyright © 2023 by Joyce A. King- All rights reserved.

The content contained within this book may not be reproduced, duplicated, or transmitted without direct written permission from the author or the publisher. Under no circumstances will any blame or legal responsibility be held against the publisher, or author, for any damages, reparation, or monetary loss due to the information contained within this book, either directly or indirectly.

Legal Notice: This book is copyright protected. It is only for personal use. You cannot amend, distribute, sell, use, quote or paraphrase any part, or the content within this book, without the consent of the author or publisher.

Disclaimer Notice: Please note the information contained within this document is for educational and entertainment purposes only. All effort has been executed to present accurate, up to date, reliable, complete information. No warranties of any kind are declared or implied. Readers acknowledge that the author is not engaged in the rendering of legal, financial, medical, or professional advice. The content within this book has been derived from various sources. Please consult a licensed professional before attempting any techniques outlined in this book. By reading this document, the reader agrees that under no circumstances is the author responsible for any losses, direct or indirect, that are incurred as a result of the use of the information contained within this document, including, but not limited to, errors, omissions, or inaccuracies.

CONTENTS

The Ultimate Guide to the Instant Vortex Plus Dual Air Fryer 9

Advantages of the Instant Vortex Plus Dual Air Fryer 9

Using the Instant Vortex Plus Dual Air Fryer 10

Cleaning and Maintenance 10

Bread And Breakfast 11

Sausage And Cream Cheese Biscuits 11

Cheddar Mushroom Taquitos 11

Egg-cilantro Cups 12

Grit And Ham Fritters 12

Quick And Easy Blueberry Muffins 13

Chicken Sausages 13

Hot Egg Cups 14

Classical French Frittata 14

Dried Fruit Beignets 15

Cinnamon French Toast 15

Zucchini Fritters 16

Creamy Broccoli Omelet 16

Air-fried Chicken Wings And Waffles 17

Italian Egg Cups 17

Home-made Potatoes With Paprika 18

Feta Stuffed Peppers With Broccoli 18

Pretzels 19

Flavorful Scrambled Eggs With Chorizo 19

Vegetable Quiche 20

Parmesan Spinach Muffins 20

Parmesan Ranch Risotto 21

Shrimp And Rice Frittata 21

Appetizers And Snacks 22

- Garlicky Cucumber Chips 22
- Fried Olives 22
- Low-carb Cheese-stuffed Jalapeño Poppers 23
- Spinach And Artichoke Dip Wontons 23
- Pesto Bruschetta 24
- Zucchini Chips With Cheese 24
- Roasted Nut Mixture 25
- Spiced Mixed Nuts 25
- Ranch Kale Chips 26
- Coconut Granola With Almond 26
- Awesome Lemony Green Beans 27
- Beef Meatballs With Chives 27
- Garlicky Radish Chips 28
- Cheesy Jalapeño Poppers 28
- Veggie Shrimp Toast 29
- Mozzarella Arancini 29
- Tasty Shrimp Bacon Wraps 30
- Mini Chicken Meatballs 30
- Homemade Chicken Drumsticks 31
- Parmesan Cauliflower Dip 31
- Tortellini With Spicy Dipping Sauce 32
- Enticing Pork Meatballs 32

Poultry Recipes 33

- Garlic Soy Chicken Thighs 33
- Za'atar Chicken Thighs 33
- Greek Chicken Kebabs 34
- Turkish Chicken Kebabs 34

Sweet And Sour Chicken Drumsticks 35

Chicken Manchurian 35

Mouthwatering Chicken Wings 36

Chicken Satay 36

Chicken Burgers With Parmesan Cheese 37

Buffalo Chicken Wings 37

Chicken And Veggies Salad 38

Barbecued Chicken Skewers 38

Southern Fried Chicken 39

Seasoned Chicken Thighs With Italian Herbs 39

Sweet-and-sour Drumsticks 40

Crispy Chicken Strips 40

Teriyaki Chicken Bowls 41

Spice Chicken With Broccoli 41

Mayo Turkey Breasts 42

Tasty Pasta Chicken 42

Roasted Chicken And Vegetable Salad 43

Marinated Chicken With Peppercorns 43

Beef, Pork & Lamb Recipes 44

Pork And Ginger Meatball Bowl 44

Beef And Cheddar Burgers 44

Avocado Buttered Flank Steak 45

Parmesan Sausage Meatballs 45

Sweet-and-sour Polish Sausage 46

Sweet And Spicy Pork Chops 46

Citrus Pork Loin Roast 47

Tomato Pork Burgers 47

Bbq Pork Chops With Vegetables 48

Cheese Ground Pork 48

Beef And Vegetable Cubes 49

Steak Fingers 49

Cheesy Beef Meatballs 50

Beer Corned Beef 50

Glazed Tender Pork Chops 51

Garlic Pork Roast 51

Unique Beef Cheeseburgers 52

Pork Tenderloin With Apple Juice 52

Lollipop Lamb Chops 53

Roasted Pork Tenderloin 53

Rosemary Lamb Chops 54

Jerk Pork Butt Pieces 54

Fish And Seafood Recipes **55**

Tuna Veggie Stir-fry 55

Old Bay Shrimp 55

Crispy Herbed Salmon 56

Easy Air Fried Salmon 56

Mustard-crusted Fish Fillets 57

Cajun Fish Tacos 57

Lime Cajun Shrimp 58

Healthy Salmon With Cardamom 58

Tuna Steak With Niçoise Salad 59

Scallops And Spring Veggies 60

Old Bay Tilapia Fillets 60

Air Fried Mussels With Parsley 61

Seasoned Breaded Shrimp 61

Crumbed Fish Fillets With Parmesan Cheese 62

Homemade Lobster Tails Ever 62

Tuna Patties 63

Coconut Shrimp 64

Red Snapper With Hot Chili Paste 64

Southwestern Prawns With Asparagus 65

Asian Swordfish 65

Seafood Spring Rolls 66

Crispy Fish Tacos 67

Vegetable Side Dishes Recipes 68

Radishes And Green Onions Mix 68

Crispy Tofu With Soy Sauce 68

Lush Summer Rolls 69

Sweet Potatoes With Tofu 69

Cheesy Roasted Tomatoes 70

Simple Turmeric Cauliflower Rice 70

Simple Pesto Gnocchi 71

Crispy Spiced Asparagus 71

Spicy Sweet Potatoes 72

Easy Rosemary Green Beans 72

Spiced Cauliflower Medley 73

Roasted Bell Peppers With Garlic 73

Mushroom Risotto Croquettes 74

Roasted Brussels Sprouts 75

Breadcrumb Crusted Agnolotti 75

Roasted Corn On The Cob 76

Corn Pakodas 76

Cheddar Tomatillos With Lettuce 77

Garlic Kale Mash 77

Fried Pickles With Mayo Sauce 78

Cheese Spinach 78

Mushroom Mozzarella Risotto 79

Desserts And Sweets 79

    Almond Pecan Muffins 79

    Cinnamon Butter Muffins 80

    Walnut Banana Split 80

    Vanilla Cobbler With Hazelnut 81

    Honey Donuts 81

    Creamy Cheesecake Bites 82

    Vanilla Custard 82

    Grilled Curried Fruit 83

    Delicious Walnut Bars 83

    Low Carb Cheesecake Muffins 84

    Peanut Butter Banana Pastry Bites 84

    Erythritol Pineapple Slices 85

    Honey-roasted Pears With Ricotta 85

    Cauliflower Rice Plum Pudding 86

    Apple Turnovers 86

    Chocolate Cake With Raspberries 87

    Cookies With Mashed Strawberry 87

    Stuffed Apples 88

    Enticing Ricotta Cheese Cake 88

    Zucchini Bars With Cream Cheese 89

    Curry Peaches, Pears, And Plums 89

    Dark Chocolate Soufflé 90

Recipe Index 91

The Ultimate Guide to the Instant Vortex Plus Dual Air Fryer

The Instant Vortex Plus Dual Air Fryer is a kitchen appliance that has taken the culinary world by storm. With its innovative dual air frying technology, it has become a go-to appliance for health-conscious individuals and food enthusiasts alike. In this comprehensive guide, we will explore the many advantages of the Instant Vortex Plus Dual Air Fryer, share some tips and tricks for using it to its full potential, and discuss how to properly clean and maintain this remarkable kitchen appliance.

Advantages of the Instant Vortex Plus Dual Air Fryer

Healthier Cooking Options: One of the standout features of the Instant Vortex Plus Dual Air Fryer is its ability to cook with significantly less oil compared to traditional frying methods. By using hot air circulation, it creates crispy and delicious dishes with a fraction of the fat content, making it an excellent choice for those looking to reduce their calorie intake and promote a healthier lifestyle.

Versatile Cooking Functions: This air fryer is not limited to just air frying; it also functions as a versatile multi-cooker. With seven pre-set cooking programs, including air fry, roast, broil, bake, reheat, dehydrate, and rotate for rotisserie, it can handle a wide range of recipes from crispy french fries to succulent rotisserie chicken.

Time and Energy Efficiency: The Instant Vortex Plus Dual Air Fryer is designed to cook food faster than traditional ovens, reducing cooking times and saving energy. Its powerful heating element and precise temperature control ensure that your meals are cooked evenly and quickly.

Easy-to-Use Controls: Operating the Instant Vortex Plus Dual Air Fryer is a breeze, thanks to its user-friendly digital display and touch-sensitive controls. You can easily adjust the temperature, cooking time, and cooking mode with just a few taps.

Large Capacity: With a spacious cooking chamber, this air fryer can accommodate larger batches of food, making it ideal for families or when entertaining guests. You can prepare enough food to satisfy everyone without the hassle of multiple cooking rounds.

Easy Cleanup: The Instant Vortex Plus Dual Air Fryer features removable, dishwasher-safe components, such as the cooking trays and rotisserie basket, which make cleanup a hassle-free experience. This means less time spent scrubbing and more time enjoying your meals.

Using the Instant Vortex Plus Dual Air Fryer

Now that we've explored the advantages of the Instant Vortex Plus Dual Air Fryer, let's delve into some essential tips and techniques for using it effectively:

Preheat for Optimal Results: Preheating your air fryer for a few minutes before cooking ensures that it reaches the desired temperature and helps your food cook evenly and become crispier.

Don't Overcrowd the Basket: To achieve the best results, avoid overcrowding the cooking basket. Leave some space between food items to allow hot air to circulate effectively.

Use a Light Coating of Oil: While the air fryer significantly reduces the amount of oil needed for cooking, a light spray or brush of oil on your ingredients can enhance flavor and texture.

Shake or Flip Food: To ensure even cooking, remember to shake or flip your food halfway through the cooking process. This helps achieve a uniform crispy texture.

Experiment with Different Recipes: The Instant Vortex Plus Dual Air Fryer is incredibly versatile. Experiment with a variety of recipes, from classic favorites to new creations. You can make anything from crispy chicken wings to homemade donuts!

Be Mindful of Temperature and Time: Pay close attention to the recommended cooking temperatures and times in your recipes. Adjust as needed to achieve your desired level of crispiness and doneness.

Cleaning and Maintenance

Proper cleaning and maintenance are crucial to prolonging the life of your Instant Vortex Plus Dual Air Fryer and ensuring it continues to perform at its best. Here are some cleaning and maintenance tips:

Allow the Appliance to Cool: Always allow the air fryer to cool down before cleaning it. The cooking trays and accessories can become very hot during use.

Remove and Clean Accessories: Take out and clean all removable parts, such as the cooking trays, rotisserie basket, and drip tray. These are usually dishwasher safe for easy cleanup.

Wipe Down the Interior: Use a damp cloth or sponge to wipe down the interior of the air fryer to remove any food residue or grease buildup. Be careful not to damage the heating element or fan.

Clean the Exterior: Wipe the exterior of the air fryer with a damp cloth. Avoid using abrasive cleaners or scouring pads, as they can scratch the surface.

Descaling the Heating Element: If you notice a buildup of mineral deposits on the heating element, you may need to descale it. Follow the manufacturer's instructions for descaling, which typically involves a mixture of water and vinegar.

Store Properly: When not in use, store your Instant Vortex Plus Dual Air Fryer in a cool, dry place. Make sure it's unplugged and free from any food debris.

Bread And Breakfast

Sausage And Cream Cheese Biscuits

Servings: 5
Cooking Time: 15 Minutes

Ingredients:
- 12 ounces chicken breakfast sausage
- 1 (6-ounce) can biscuits
- ⅛ cup cream cheese

Directions:
1. Form the sausage into 5 small patties.
2. Place the sausage patties in the air fryer. Cook for 5 minutes.
3. Open the air fryer. Flip the patties. Cook for an additional 5 minutes.
4. Remove the cooked sausages from the air fryer.
5. Separate the biscuit dough into 5 biscuits.
6. Place the biscuits in the air fryer. Cook for 3 minutes.
7. Open the air fryer. Flip the biscuits. Cook for an additional 2 minutes.
8. Remove the cooked biscuits from the air fryer.
9. Split each biscuit in half. Spread 1 teaspoon of cream cheese onto the bottom of each biscuit. Top with a sausage patty and the other half of the biscuit, and serve.

Cheddar Mushroom Taquitos

Servings: 8
Cooking Time: 20 Minutes

Ingredients:
- 8 whole-wheat tortillas
- 2–3 king oyster mushrooms
- 1 cup of shredded cheddar cheese
- 1 tablespoon of lime juice
- ⅛ cup of olive oil
- ¼ tablespoon of chili powder
- 1 teaspoon of ground cumin
- 1 teaspoon of paprika
- ½ teaspoon of dried oregano
- ½ teaspoon of garlic powder
- ¼ teaspoon of salt
- ¼ teaspoon of black pepper
- ¼ teaspoon of onion powder

Directions:
1. Clean oyster mushrooms before using.
2. Cut them lengthwise into ⅛-inch-thick slices.
3. Mix chili, cumin, paprika, oregano, garlic, salt, black pepper, and onion powder in a suitable mixing bowl.
4. Add lime juice with oil and mix.
5. Place sliced mushroom into the bowl and rub with spices.
6. At 350 degrees F/ 175 degrees C, preheat your air fryer.
7. Air fry the mushroom in the air fryer for 7–10 minutes almost.
8. Divide the cooked mushrooms between all the tortillas.
9. Add shredded cheese and make a thin roll from each stuffed tortilla.
10. Spray all rolled tortillas with some oil and Air fry for almost 10 minutes.
11. Serve.

Egg-cilantro Cups

Servings: 4
Cooking Time: 14 Minutes
Ingredients:
- 4 eggs
- 1 tablespoon cilantro, chopped
- 4 tablespoon half and half
- 1 cup cheddar cheese, shredded
- 1 cup vegetables, diced
- Black pepper
- Salt

Directions:
1. Sprinkle 4 ramekins with cooking spray and set aside.
2. In a suitable mixing bowl, whisk eggs with cilantro, half and half, vegetables, ½ cup cheese, black pepper, and salt.
3. Pour egg mixture into the 4 ramekins.
4. Place the prepared ramekins in air fryer basket and cook at almost 300 degrees F/ 150 degrees C for 12 minutes.
5. Top with remaining ½ cup cheese and cook for 2 minutes more at 400 degrees F/ 205 degrees C.
6. Serve and enjoy.

Grit And Ham Fritters

Servings:8
Cooking Time: 20 Minutes
Ingredients:
- 4 cups water
- 1 cup quick-cooking grits
- ¼ teaspoon salt
- 2 tablespoons butter
- 2 cups grated Cheddar cheese, divided
- 1 cup finely diced ham
- 1 tablespoon chopped chives
- Salt and freshly ground black pepper, to taste
- 1 egg, beaten
- 2 cups panko bread crumbs
- Cooking spray

Directions:
1. Bring the water to a boil in a saucepan. Whisk in the grits and ¼ teaspoon of salt, and cook for 7 minutes until the grits are soft. Remove the pan from the heat and stir in the butter and 1 cup of the grated Cheddar cheese. Transfer the grits to a bowl and let them cool for 10 to 15 minutes.
2. Stir the ham, chives and the rest of the cheese into the grits and season with salt and pepper to taste. Add the beaten egg and refrigerate the mixture for 30 minutes.
3. Put the panko bread crumbs in a shallow dish. Measure out ¼-cup portions of the grits mixture and shape them into patties. Coat all sides of the patties with the panko bread crumbs, patting them with the hands so the crumbs adhere to the patties. You should have about 16 patties. Spritz both sides of the patties with cooking spray.
4. Preheat the air fryer to 400ºF (204ºC).
5. In batches of 5 or 6, air fry the fritters for 8 minutes. Using a flat spatula, flip the fritters over and air fry for another 4 minutes.
6. Serve hot.

Quick And Easy Blueberry Muffins

Servings: 8
Cooking Time: 12 Minutes

Ingredients:
- 1⅓ cups flour
- ½ cup sugar
- 2 teaspoons baking powder
- ¼ teaspoon salt
- ⅓ cup canola oil
- 1 egg
- ½ cup milk
- ⅔ cup blueberries, fresh or frozen and thawed

Directions:
1. Preheat the air fryer to 330°F (166°C).
2. In a medium bowl, stir together flour, sugar, baking powder, and salt.
3. In a separate bowl, combine oil, egg, and milk and mix well.
4. Add egg mixture to dry ingredients and stir just until moistened.
5. Gently stir in the blueberries.
6. Spoon batter evenly into parchment-paper-lined muffin cups.
7. Put 4 muffin cups in air fryer basket and bake for 12 minutes or until tops spring back when touched lightly.
8. Repeat previous step to bake remaining muffins.
9. Serve immediately.

Chicken Sausages

Servings: 8
Cooking Time: 8 To 12 Minutes

Ingredients:
- 1 Granny Smith apple, peeled and finely chopped
- ⅓ cup minced onion
- 3 tablespoons ground almonds
- 2 garlic cloves, minced
- 1 egg white
- 2 tablespoons apple juice
- ⅛ teaspoon freshly ground black pepper
- 1 pound ground chicken breast

Directions:
1. In a medium bowl, thoroughly mix the apple, onion, almonds, garlic, egg white, apple juice, and pepper.
2. With your hands, gently work the chicken breast into the apple mixture until combined.
3. Form the mixture into 8 patties. Put the patties into the air fryer basket. You may need to cook them in batches. Air-fry for 8 to 12 minutes, or until the patties reach an internal temperature of 165°F on a meat thermometer (see Tip). Serve.

Hot Egg Cups

Servings: 6
Cooking Time: 3 Minutes
Ingredients:
- 6 eggs, beaten
- 2 jalapenos, sliced
- 2 ounces' bacon, chopped, cooked
- ½ teaspoon salt
- ½ teaspoon chili powder
- Cooking spray

Directions:
1. Spray cooking spray onto the inside of the silicone egg molds.
2. Mix up sliced jalapeno, bacon, beaten eggs, chili powder, and salt in the mixing bowl.
3. Gently whisk together the liquid and pour into the egg molds.
4. Before cooking, heat your air fryer to 400 degrees F/ 205 degrees C.
5. Place the egg cups inside the air fryer and close the air fryer.
6. Cook in your air fryer for 3 minutes.
7. Then cool the cooked cups for 2-3 minutes.
8. Remove from the silicone molds and serve.

Classical French Frittata

Servings: 3
Cooking Time: 18 Minutes
Ingredients:
- 3 eggs
- 1 tablespoon heavy cream
- 1 teaspoon Herbs de Provence
- 1 teaspoon almond butter, softened
- 2 ounces Provolone cheese, grated

Directions:
1. Before cooking, heat your air fryer to 365 degrees F/ 185 degrees C.
2. Whisk the 3 eggs together in a medium bowl and then add the heavy cream. Whisk again with a hand whisker until smooth.
3. Then add herbs de Provence and the grated cheese.
4. Gently stir the egg mixture.
5. Using almond butter, grease the baking pan.
6. Then pour the egg mixture evenly on the baking pan.
7. Cook in the preheated air fryer for 18 minutes.
8. When it has preheated, cool to room temperature, and slice and serve.

Dried Fruit Beignets

Servings: 16
Cooking Time: 5 To 8 Minutes

Ingredients:

- 1 teaspoon active quick-rising dry yeast
- ⅓ cup buttermilk
- 3 tablespoons packed brown sugar
- 1 egg
- 1½ cups whole-wheat pastry flour
- 3 tablespoons chopped dried cherries
- 3 tablespoons chopped golden raisins
- 2 tablespoons unsalted butter, melted
- Powdered sugar, for dusting (optional)

Directions:
1. In a medium bowl, mix the yeast with 3 tablespoons of water. Let it stand for 5 minutes, or until it bubbles.
2. Stir in the buttermilk, brown sugar, and egg until well mixed.
3. Stir in the pastry flour until combined.
4. With your hands, work the cherries and raisins into the dough. Let the mixture stand for 15 minutes.
5. Pat the dough into an 8-by-8-inch square and cut into 16 pieces. Gently shape each piece into a ball.
6. Drizzle the balls with the melted butter. Place them in a single layer in the air fryer basket so they don't touch. You may have to cook these in batches. Air-fry for 5 to 8 minutes, or until puffy and golden brown.
7. Dust with powdered sugar before serving, if desired.

Cinnamon French Toast

Servings: 2
Cooking Time: 9 Minutes

Ingredients:

- ⅓ cup almond flour
- 1 egg, beaten
- ¼ teaspoon baking powder
- 2 teaspoons Erythritol
- ¼ teaspoon vanilla extract
- 1 teaspoon cream cheese
- ¼ teaspoon ground cinnamon
- 1 teaspoon ghee, melted

Directions:
1. Mix up baking powder, ground cinnamon, and almond flour in a mixing bowl.
2. Add in vanilla extract, cream cheese, egg, and ghee and stir together with a fork until smooth.
3. Place baking paper on the bottom of the mugs.
4. Add in almond flour mixture and use a fork to flatten well.
5. Before cooking, heat your air fryer to 255 degrees F/ 125 degrees C.
6. Transfer the mugs with toasts inside your air fryer basket.
7. Cook in your air fryer for 9 minutes.
8. When cooked, cool for a while. To serve, sprinkle Erythritol on the toasts.

Zucchini Fritters

Servings: 4
Cooking Time: 8 Minutes
Ingredients:
- 2 zucchinis, grated
- 3 tablespoons almond flour
- 1 medium egg, beaten
- ¼ teaspoon salt
- ¼ teaspoon ground black pepper
- ¼ teaspoon minced garlic
- 1 tablespoon spring onions, chopped
- ¼ teaspoon chili flakes

Directions:
1. In a bowl, add the grated zucchinis and the almond flour.
2. Then place in the salt, ground black pepper, minced garlic, chili flakes, green peas, and egg.
3. Using a fork stir together the ingredients until homogenous.
4. Before cooking, heat your air fryer to 365 degrees F/ 185 degrees C.
5. To make the fritters, put the mixture on the baking paper with a spoon.
6. Transfer into the preheated air fryer and cook for 8 minutes. Halfway through cooking, flip the fritters to the other side.
7. Serve.

Creamy Broccoli Omelet

Servings: 4
Cooking Time: 14 Minutes
Ingredients:
- 4 eggs, beaten
- 1 tablespoon cream cheese
- ½ teaspoon chili flakes
- ½ cup broccoli florets, chopped
- ¼ teaspoon salt
- ¼ cup heavy cream
- ¼ teaspoon white pepper
- Cooking spray

Directions:
1. In a large bowl, place the beaten eggs, salt, white pepper, and chili flakes.
2. With a hand whisker, stir together until the salt is dissolved.
3. Place the heavy cream and cream cheese in the bowl and again stir until homogenous.
4. Then add the broccoli florets.
5. Before cooking, heat your air fryer to 375 degrees F/ 190 degrees C.
6. Using cooking spray, spray the air fryer basket from inside.
7. Pour in the egg liquid and cook in the air fryer for 14 minutes.

Air-fried Chicken Wings And Waffles

Servings: 4
Cooking Time: 20 Minutes

Ingredients:
- 8 whole chicken wings
- 1 teaspoon garlic powder
- Chicken seasoning or rub
- Black pepper
- ½ cup all-purpose flour
- Cooking oil
- 8 frozen waffles
- Maple syrup

Directions:
1. At 400 degrees F/ 205 degrees C, preheat your air fryer.
2. In a suitable bowl, spice the chicken with the garlic powder and chicken seasoning and black pepper to flavor.
3. Put the chicken to a sealable plastic bag and add the flour. Shake to thoroughly coat the chicken.
4. Grease its air fryer basket with cooking oil.
5. Place chicken in the greased air fryer basket and air fry for 20 minutes while tossing occasionally.
6. Transfer the air fried chicken wings to a plate and add frozen waffles to the air fryer and cook for almost 6 minutes.
7. Serve the air fried chicken with waffles.

Italian Egg Cups

Servings:4
Cooking Time: 10 Minutes

Ingredients:
- Olive oil
- 1 cup marinara sauce
- 4 eggs
- 4 tablespoons shredded mozzarella cheese
- 4 teaspoons grated Parmesan cheese
- Salt
- Freshly ground black pepper
- Chopped fresh basil, for garnish

Directions:
1. Lightly spray 4 individual ramekins with olive oil.
2. Pour ¼ cup of marinara sauce into each ramekin.
3. Crack one egg into each ramekin on top of the marinara sauce.
4. Sprinkle 1 tablespoon of mozzarella and 1 tablespoon of Parmesan on top of each egg. Season with salt and pepper.
5. Cover each ramekin with aluminum foil. Place two of the ramekins in the fryer basket.
6. Air fry for 5 minutes and remove the aluminum foil. Air fry until the top is lightly browned and the egg white is cooked, another 2 to 4 minutes. If you prefer the yolk to be firmer, cook for 3 to 5 more minutes.
7. Repeat with the remaining two ramekins. Garnish with basil and serve.

Home-made Potatoes With Paprika

Servings: 4
Cooking Time: 25 Minutes

Ingredients:

- 3 large russet potatoes
- 1 tablespoon canola oil
- 1 tablespoon extra-virgin olive oil
- 1 teaspoon paprika
- Salt
- Black pepper
- 1 cup chopped onion
- 1 cup chopped red bell pepper
- 1 cup chopped green bell pepper

Directions:

1. Cut the potatoes into ½-inch cubes.
2. Place the potatoes in a suitable bowl of cold water and allow them to soak for about 30 to 60 minutes.
3. Dry out the potatoes and wipe thoroughly with paper towels.
4. Return them to the empty bowl.
5. Add the canola and olive oils, paprika, and black pepper and salt to flavor.
6. Toss to fully coat the potatoes.
7. Transfer the potatoes to the air fryer.
8. Cook for 20 minutes, shaking the air fryer basket every 5 minutes a total of 4 times.
9. Put the onion and red and green bell peppers to the air fryer basket. Fry for an additional 3 to 4 minutes, or until the potatoes are cooked through and the black peppers are soft.
10. Cool before serving.

Feta Stuffed Peppers With Broccoli

Servings: 2
Cooking Time: 40 Minutes

Ingredients:

- 4 eggs
- ½ cup cheddar cheese, grated
- 2 bell peppers cut in ½ and remove seeds
- ½ teaspoon garlic powder
- 1 teaspoon dried thyme
- ¼ cup feta cheese, crumbled
- ½ cup broccoli, cooked
- ¼ teaspoon black pepper
- ½ teaspoon salt

Directions:

1. At 325 degrees F/ 160 degrees C, preheat your air fryer.
2. Stuff feta and broccoli into the bell peppers halved.
3. Beat egg in a suitable bowl with seasoning and pour egg mixture into the black pepper halved over feta and broccoli.
4. Place bell pepper halved into the air fryer basket and cook for 35-40 minutes.
5. Top with cheddar, grated cheese and cook until cheese melted.
6. Serve and enjoy.

Pretzels

Servings: 24
Cooking Time: 6 Minutes

Ingredients:

- 2 teaspoons yeast
- 1 cup water, warm
- 1 teaspoon sugar
- 1 teaspoon salt
- 2½ cups all-purpose flour
- 2 tablespoons butter, melted, plus more as needed
- 1 cup boiling water
- 1 tablespoon baking soda
- Coarse sea salt, to taste

Directions:

1. Combine the yeast and water in a small bowl. Combine the sugar, salt and flour in the bowl of a stand mixer. With the mixer running and using the dough hook, drizzle in the yeast mixture and melted butter and knead dough until smooth and elastic, about 10 minutes. Shape into a ball and let the dough rise for 1 hour.
2. Punch the dough down to release any air and divide the dough into 24 portions.
3. Roll each portion into a skinny rope using both hands on the counter and rolling from the center to the ends of the rope. Spin the rope into a pretzel shape (or tie the rope into a knot) and place the tied pretzels on a parchment lined baking sheet.
4. Preheat the air fryer to 350°F (177°C).
5. Combine the boiling water and baking soda in a shallow bowl and whisk to dissolve. Let the water cool so you can put the hands in it. Working in batches, dip the pretzels (top side down) into the baking soda mixture and let them soak for 30 seconds to a minute. Then remove the pretzels carefully and return them (top side up) to the baking sheet. Sprinkle the coarse salt on the top.
6. Air fry in batches for 3 minutes per side. When the pretzels are finished, brush them generously with the melted butter and enjoy them warm.

Flavorful Scrambled Eggs With Chorizo

Servings: 2
Cooking Time: 13 Minutes

Ingredients:

- 1 dash of Spanish paprika
- 1 dash of oregano
- 3 large eggs, beaten
- 1 tablespoon olive oil
- ½ zucchini, sliced
- ½ chorizo sausage, sliced

Directions:

1. Prepare all the recipe ingredients.
2. At 350 degrees F/ 175 degrees C, preheat your air fryer. Fry the zucchini in olive oil, season with salt and cook for 2-3 minutes.
3. Add chorizo to the zucchini and cook for another 5-6 minutes.
4. Fill with the egg mixture and send it back to the air fryer for 5 minutes, take out the basket and stir for every minute until tender.
5. Serve and Enjoy.

Vegetable Quiche

Servings: 2 Servings
Cooking Time: 20 Minutes

Ingredients:

- 2 large eggs
- ½ cup of heavy cream
- 6–8 small broccoli florets
- 2 tablespoons of grated cheddar
- Pinch of salt and black pepper, to taste

Directions:

1. Preheat your air fryer to 325°F. Lightly grease two 5-inch ceramic dishes with oil.
2. Put eggs, heavy cream, salt, and black pepper into a mixing bowl. Whisk it well.
3. Put broccoli florets on the dish's bottom and pour the egg mixture over them.
4. Cook it at 325°F for 10 minutes.* Check the readiness using a toothpick; it should come out clean after inserting in the center.
5. Serve warm and enjoy your Vegetable Quiche!

Parmesan Spinach Muffins

Servings: 4
Cooking Time: 15 Minutes

Ingredients:

- 2 eggs, whisked
- Cooking spray
- 1 and ½ cups coconut milk
- 1 tablespoon baking powder
- 4 ounces baby spinach, chopped
- 2 ounces parmesan cheese, grated
- 3 ounces almond flour

Directions:

1. Grease the muffin molds with cooking spray.
2. Mix the whisked eggs, coconut milk, baking powder, baby spinach, parmesan cheese, and almond flour together in a mixing bowl.
3. Transfer onto the greased molds.
4. Cook in your air fryer at 380 degrees F/ 195 degrees C for 15 minutes.
5. When the cooking time is up, serve on plates.
6. Enjoy your breakfast.

Parmesan Ranch Risotto

Servings: 2
Cooking Time: 30 Minutes

Ingredients:

- 1 tablespoon olive oil
- 1 clove garlic, minced
- 1 tablespoon unsalted butter
- 1 onion, diced
- ¾ cup Arborio rice
- 2 cups chicken stock, boiling
- ½ cup Parmesan cheese, grated

Directions:

1. Preheat the air fryer to 390°F (199°C).
2. Grease a round baking tin with olive oil and stir in the garlic, butter, and onion.
3. Transfer the tin to the air fryer and bake for 4 minutes. Add the rice and bake for 4 more minutes.
4. Turn the air fryer to 320°F (160°C) and pour in the chicken stock. Cover and bake for 22 minutes.
5. Scatter with cheese and serve.

Shrimp And Rice Frittata

Servings: 4
Cooking Time: 15 Minutes

Ingredients:

- 4 eggs
- Pinch salt
- ½ teaspoon dried basil
- Nonstick cooking spray
- ½ cup cooked rice
- ½ cup chopped cooked shrimp
- ½ cup baby spinach
- ½ cup grated Monterey Jack or Cojack cheese

Directions:

1. In a small bowl, beat the eggs with the salt and basil until frothy. Spray a 6-by-6-by-2-inch pan with nonstick cooking spray.
2. Combine the rice, shrimp, and spinach in the prepared pan. Pour the eggs in and sprinkle with the cheese.
3. Bake for 14 to 18 minutes or until the frittata is puffed and golden brown.

Appetizers And Snacks
Garlicky Cucumber Chips

Servings: 12
Cooking Time: 11 Minutes
Ingredients:
- 1 pound cucumber
- ½ teaspoon garlic powder
- 1 tablespoon paprika
- 1 teaspoon salt

Directions:
1. Wash cucumber and slice thinly using a mandolin slicer.
2. At 370 degrees F/ 185 degrees C, preheat your air fryer.
3. Add cucumber slices into the air fryer basket and sprinkle with garlic powder, paprika, and salt.
4. Toss well and cook for 11 minutes. Shake halfway through.
5. Serve and enjoy.

Fried Olives

Servings: 4
Cooking Time: 10 Minutes
Ingredients:
- 1 (5½-ounce) jar pitted green olives
- ½ cup all-purpose flour
- Salt
- Pepper
- ½ cup bread crumbs
- 1 egg
- Cooking oil

Directions:
1. Remove the olives from the jar and dry thoroughly with paper towels.
2. In a small bowl, combine the flour with salt and pepper to taste. Place the bread crumbs in another small bowl. In a third small bowl, beat the egg.
3. Spray the air fryer basket with cooking oil.
4. Dip the olives in the flour, then the egg, and then the bread crumbs.
5. Place the breaded olives in the air fryer. It is okay to stack them. Spray the olives with cooking oil. Cook for 6 minutes.
6. Open the air fryer. Flip the olives. Because olives are small, I prefer to flip them instead of shaking to maintain the breading.
7. Cook for an additional 2 minutes, or until brown and crisp.
8. Cool before serving.

Low-carb Cheese-stuffed Jalapeño Poppers

Servings: 5
Cooking Time: 5 Minutes

Ingredients:
- 10 jalapeño peppers
- 6 ounces cream cheese
- ¼ cup shredded Cheddar cheese
- 2 tablespoons panko bread crumbs
- Cooking oil

Directions:
1. I recommend you wear gloves while handling jalapeños. Halve the jalapeños lengthwise. Remove the seeds and the white membrane. (Save these if you prefer spicy poppers; see Variation tip.)
2. Place the cream cheese in a small, microwave-safe bowl. Microwave for 15 seconds to soften.
3. Remove the bowl from the microwave. Add the Cheddar cheese. Mix well.
4. Stuff each of the jalapeño halves with the cheese mixture, then sprinkle the panko bread crumbs on top of each popper.
5. Place the poppers in the air fryer. Spray them with cooking oil. Cook for 5 minutes.
6. Cool before serving.

Spinach And Artichoke Dip Wontons

Servings: 20
Cooking Time: 40 Minutes

Ingredients:
- 6 ounces cream cheese
- ¼ cup sour cream
- ¼ cup shredded Parmesan cheese
- ¼ cup shredded mozzarella cheese
- 5 ounces frozen chopped spinach, thawed and drained
- 6 ounces marinated artichoke hearts, drained
- 2 garlic cloves, chopped
- Salt
- Pepper
- 20 wonton wrappers
- Cooking oil

Directions:
1. In a small, microwave-safe bowl, heat the cream cheese in the microwave for 20 seconds to soften.
2. In a medium bowl, combine the cream cheese, sour cream, Parmesan, mozzarella, spinach, artichoke hearts, garlic, and salt and pepper to taste. Stir to mix well.
3. Lay out the wonton wrappers on a work surface. A clean table or large cutting board works well.
4. Scoop 1½ teaspoons of the artichoke mixture onto each wrapper. Be careful not to overfill.
5. Fold each wrapper diagonally to form a triangle. Bring the two bottom corners up toward each other. Do not close the wrapper yet. Bring up the two open sides and push out any air. Squeeze the open edges together to seal.
6. Place the wontons in the air fryer basket and cook in batches, or stack (see Air fryer cooking tip). Spray the wontons with cooking oil. Cook for 10 minutes.
7. Remove the basket and flip the wontons. Return to the air fryer and cook for an additional 5 to 8 minutes, until the wontons have reached your desired level of golden-brown crispiness.
8. If cooking in batches, remove the cooked wontons from the air fryer, then repeat steps 6 and 7 for the remaining wontons.
9. Cool before serving.

Pesto Bruschetta

Servings: 4
Cooking Time: 4 To 8 Minutes
Ingredients:
- 8 slices French bread, ½ inch thick
- 2 tablespoons softened butter
- 1 cup shredded mozzarella cheese
- ½ cup basil pesto
- 1 cup chopped grape tomatoes
- 2 green onions, thinly sliced

Directions:
1. Spread the bread with the butter and place butter-side up in the air fryer basket. Bake for 3 to 5 minutes or until the bread is light golden brown.
2. Remove the bread from the basket and top each piece with some of the cheese. Return to the basket in batches and bake until the cheese melts, about 1 to 3 minutes.
3. Meanwhile, combine the pesto, tomatoes, and green onions in a small bowl.
4. When the cheese has melted, remove the bread from the air fryer and place on a serving plate. Top each slice with some of the pesto mixture and serve.

Zucchini Chips With Cheese

Servings: 8
Cooking Time: 13 Minutes
Ingredients:
- 2 zucchinis, thinly sliced
- 4 tablespoons almond flour
- 2 oz. Parmesan
- 2 eggs, beaten
- ½ teaspoon white pepper
- Cooking spray

Directions:
1. Prepare your clean air fryer and preheat it to 355 degrees F/ 180 degrees C.
2. Thoroughly mix up almond flour, Parmesan and white pepper in a large bowl.
3. After that, dip the zucchini slices in the egg and coat in the almond flour mixture.
4. Place the prepared zucchini slices in the preheated air fryer and cook them for 10 minutes.
5. Flip the vegetables on another side and cook them for 3 minutes more or until crispy.
6. Serve and enjoy.

Roasted Nut Mixture

Servings: 6
Cooking Time: 20 Minutes

Ingredients:

- ½ cup walnuts
- ½ cup pecans
- ½ cup almonds
- 1 egg white
- 1 packet stevia
- ½-tablespoon ground cinnamon
- A pinch of cayenne pepper

Directions:

1. Mix up all of the ingredients in a bowl.
2. Arrange the nuts to the basket in the preheated air fryer (you can lay a piece of baking paper).
3. Cook the nuts for about 20 minutes at 320 degrees F/ 160 degrees C, stirring once halfway through.
4. Once done, transfer the hot nuts in a glass or steel bowl and serve.

Spiced Mixed Nuts

Servings: 2
Cooking Time: 6 Minutes

Ingredients:

- ½ cup raw cashews
- ½ cup raw pecan halves
- ½ cup raw walnut halves
- ½ cup raw whole almonds
- 2 tablespoons olive oil
- 1 tablespoon light brown sugar
- 1 teaspoon chopped fresh rosemary leaves
- 1 teaspoon chopped fresh thyme leaves
- 1 teaspoon kosher salt
- ½ teaspoon ground coriander
- ¼ teaspoon onion powder
- ¼ teaspoon freshly ground black pepper
- ⅛ teaspoon garlic powder

Directions:

1. Preheat the air fryer to 350°F (177°C).
2. In a large bowl, combine all the ingredients and toss until the nuts are evenly coated in the herbs, spices, and sugar.
3. Scrape the nuts and seasonings into the air fryer and air fry for 6 minutes, or until golden brown and fragrant, shaking the basket halfway through.
4. Transfer the cocktail nuts to a bowl and serve warm.

Ranch Kale Chips

Servings: 4
Cooking Time: 5 Minutes

Ingredients:
- 4 cups kale, stemmed
- 1 tablespoon nutritional yeast flakes
- 2 teaspoons ranch seasoning
- 2 tablespoons olive oil
- ¼ teaspoon salt

Directions:
1. Add all the recipe ingredients into the suitable mixing bowl and toss well.
2. Grease its air fryer basket with cooking spray.
3. Add kale in air fryer basket and cook for 4 to 5 minutes at 370 degrees F/ 185 degrees C. Shake halfway through.
4. Serve and enjoy.

Coconut Granola With Almond

Servings: 4
Cooking Time: 12 Minutes

Ingredients:
- 1 teaspoon monk fruit
- 1 teaspoon almond butter
- 1 teaspoon coconut oil
- 2 tablespoons almonds, chopped
- 1 teaspoon pumpkin puree
- ½ teaspoon pumpkin pie spices
- 2 tablespoons coconut flakes
- 2 tablespoons pumpkin seeds, crushed
- 1 teaspoon hemp seeds
- 1 teaspoon flax seeds
- Cooking spray

Directions:
1. Mix up almond butter and coconut oil in a big bowl and then microwave the mixture until melted.
2. Continue to mix up the pumpkin spices, pumpkin seeds, monk fruit, coconut flakes, hemp seeds and flax seeds in another suitable bowl.
3. Add the pumpkin puree and melted coconut oil, then stir the mixture until homogenous.
4. Arrange the pumpkin mixture on the baking paper and make the shape of square, then cut the square on the serving bars and transfer in the air fryer.
5. Cook them for 12 minutes at 350 degrees F/ 175 degrees C.
6. Once done, serve and enjoy.

Awesome Lemony Green Beans

Servings: 4
Cooking Time: 12 Minutes

Ingredients:
- 1 lemon, juiced
- 1-pound green beans, washed and destemmed
- ¼ teaspoon extra virgin olive oil
- Salt to taste
- Black pepper to taste

Directions:
1. At 400 degrees F/ 205 degrees C, preheat your air fryer.
2. Put the green beans in your air fryer basket and drizzle the lemon juice over them.
3. Sprinkle on the black pepper and salt.
4. Pour in the oil, and toss to coat the green beans well.
5. Cook for almost 10-12 minutes and serve warm.

Beef Meatballs With Chives

Servings: 6
Cooking Time: 20 Minutes

Ingredients:
- 1 pound beef meat, ground
- 1 teaspoon onion powder
- 1 teaspoon garlic powder
- A pinch of salt and black pepper
- 2 tablespoons chives, chopped Cooking spray

Directions:
1. In addition to the cooking spray, mix the other ingredients well in a bowl and shape medium meatballs out of this mix.
2. Place the balls in the basket of your air fryer and oil them.
3. Cook for 20 minutes at 360 degrees F/ 180 degrees C.
4. When done, serve as an appetizer.

Garlicky Radish Chips

Servings: 1
Cooking Time: 10 Minutes
Ingredients:
- 2 cups water
- 1 pound radishes
- ½ teaspoon garlic powder
- ¼ teaspoon onion powder
- 2 tablespoons coconut oil, melted

Directions:
1. Boil the water over the stove.
2. Slice off the radish's tops and bottoms and, using a mandolin, shave into thin slices of equal size.
3. Put the radish chips in the pot of boiling water and allow to cook for 5 minutes, ensuring they become translucent.
4. Take care when removing from the water and place them on a paper towel to dry.
5. Add the radish chips, garlic powder, onion powder, and melted coconut oil into a bowl and toss to coat.
6. Cook at almost 320 degrees F/ 160 degrees C for 5 minutes.
7. Serve.

Cheesy Jalapeño Poppers

Servings: 4
Cooking Time: 10 Minutes
Ingredients:
- 8 jalapeño peppers
- ½ cup whipped cream cheese
- ¼ cup shredded Cheddar cheese

Directions:
1. Preheat the air fryer to 360°F (182°C).
2. Use a paring knife to carefully cut off the jalapeño tops, then scoop out the ribs and seeds. Set aside.
3. In a medium bowl, combine the whipped cream cheese and shredded Cheddar cheese. Place the mixture in a sealable plastic bag, and using a pair of scissors, cut off one corner from the bag. Gently squeeze some cream cheese mixture into each pepper until almost full.
4. Place a piece of parchment paper on the bottom of the air fryer basket and place the poppers on top, distributing evenly. Air fry for 10 minutes.
5. Allow the poppers to cool for 5 to 10 minutes before serving.

Veggie Shrimp Toast

Servings:4
Cooking Time: 3 To 6 Minutes

Ingredients:
- 8 large raw shrimp, peeled and finely chopped
- 1 egg white
- 2 garlic cloves, minced
- 3 tablespoons minced red bell pepper
- 1 medium celery stalk, minced
- 2 tablespoons cornstarch
- ¼ teaspoon Chinese five-spice powder
- 3 slices firm thin-sliced no-sodium whole-wheat bread

Directions:
1. Preheat the air fryer to 350ºF (177ºC).
2. In a small bowl, stir together the shrimp, egg white, garlic, red bell pepper, celery, cornstarch, and five-spice powder. Top each slice of bread with one-third of the shrimp mixture, spreading it evenly to the edges. With a sharp knife, cut each slice of bread into 4 strips.
3. Place the shrimp toasts in the air fryer basket in a single layer. You may need to cook them in batches. Air fry for 3 to 6 minutes, until crisp and golden brown.
4. Serve hot.

Mozzarella Arancini

Servings:16
Cooking Time: 8 To 11 Minutes

Ingredients:
- 2 cups cooked rice, cooled
- 2 eggs, beaten
- 1½ cups panko bread crumbs, divided
- ½ cup grated Parmesan cheese
- 2 tablespoons minced fresh basil
- 16 ¾-inch cubes Mozzarella cheese
- 2 tablespoons olive oil

Directions:
1. Preheat the air fryer to 400ºF (204ºC).
2. In a medium bowl, combine the rice, eggs, ½ cup of the bread crumbs, Parmesan cheese, and basil. Form this mixture into 16 1½-inch balls.
3. Poke a hole in each of the balls with your finger and insert a Mozzarella cube. Form the rice mixture firmly around the cheese.
4. On a shallow plate, combine the remaining 1 cup of the bread crumbs with the olive oil and mix well. Roll the rice balls in the bread crumbs to coat.
5. Air fry the arancini in batches for 8 to 11 minutes or until golden brown.
6. Serve hot.

Tasty Shrimp Bacon Wraps

Servings: 8-10
Cooking Time: 8 Minutes

Ingredients:

- ½ teaspoon red pepper flakes, crushed
- 1 tablespoon salt
- 1 teaspoon chili powder
- 1 ¼ pounds shrimp, peeled and deveined
- 1 teaspoon paprika
- ½ teaspoon black pepper, ground
- 1 tablespoon shallot powder
- ¼ teaspoon cumin powder
- 1 ¼ pounds thin bacon slices

Directions:

1. Prepare your clean air fryer.
2. Preheat the air fryer for 4 to 5 minutes at 360 degrees F/ 180 degrees C.
3. Oil or spray the air-frying basket gently.
4. Mix the shrimp and seasoning in a medium-size bowl thoroughly, until they are coated well.
5. Use a slice of bacon to wrap around the shrimps and use a toothpick to secure them. Then place them in the refrigerator and cool for 30 minutes.
6. Add the shrimps to the basket and then put the basket in the air fryer.
7. Cook the shrimps for 8 minutes.
8. You can serve with cocktail sticks or your choice of dip (optional).

Mini Chicken Meatballs

Servings:16
Cooking Time:13 To 20 Minutes

Ingredients:

- 2 teaspoons olive oil
- ¼ cup minced onion
- ¼ cup minced red bell pepper
- 2 vanilla wafers, crushed
- 1 egg white
- ½ teaspoon dried thyme
- ½ pound ground chicken breast (see Tip)

Directions:

1. In a 6-by-2-inch pan, mix the olive oil, onion, and red bell pepper. Put the pan in the air fryer. Cook for 3 to 5 minutes, or until the vegetables are tender.
2. In a medium bowl, mix the cooked vegetables, crushed wafers, egg white, and thyme until well combined
3. Mix in the chicken, gently but thoroughly, until everything is combined.
4. Form the mixture into 16 meatballs and place them in the air fryer basket. Air-fry for 10 to 15 minutes, or until the meatballs reach an internal temperature of 165°F on a meat thermometer. Serve immediately.

Homemade Chicken Drumsticks

Servings: 5
Cooking Time: 20 Minutes

Ingredients:

- For the Sauce:
- 1 tablespoon Worcestershire sauce
- 1 tablespoon red wine vinegar
- 1 tablespoon olive oil
- 1 ½ cup ketchup
- 1 tablespoon mustard
- 1 tablespoon brown sugar
- 1 tablespoon honey
- ½ teaspoon granulated garlic
- Salt and pepper, to taste
- ⅛ teaspoon ground allspice
- ¼ cup water
- For the Chicken Drumsticks:
- 2 lb. chicken drumsticks
- ⅓ teaspoon Kosher salt
- ⅓ cup fresh parsley, finely chopped

Directions:

1. Sauté all the sauce ingredients in a sauté pan over medium-high heat and let them simmer a few minutes.
2. Reduce the heat and cook until thickens.
3. In your air fryer, cook the chicken drumsticks at 390 degrees F/ 200 degrees C for 15 minutes. When cooked, season them with Kosher salt.
4. Serve warm with the prepared sauce and top with finely chopped parsley. Bon appétit!

Parmesan Cauliflower Dip

Servings: 10
Cooking Time: 45 Minutes

Ingredients:

- 1 cauliflower head, cut into florets
- 1 ½ cups parmesan cheese, shredded
- 2 tablespoons green onions, chopped
- 2 garlic clove
- 1 teaspoon Worcestershire sauce
- ½ cup sour cream
- ¾ cup mayonnaise
- 8 ounces cream cheese, softened
- 2 tablespoons olive oil

Directions:

1. Toss cauliflower florets with olive oil.
2. Add cauliflower florets into the air fryer basket and cook at almost 390 degrees F/ 200 degrees C for 20-25 minutes.
3. Add cooked cauliflower, 1 cup of parmesan cheese, cream cheese, green onion, garlic, Worcestershire sauce, sour cream, and mayonnaise into the food processor and process until smooth.
4. Transfer cauliflower mixture into the 7-inch dish and top with remaining parmesan cheese.
5. Place dish in air fryer basket and Cook at almost 360 degrees F/ 180 degrees C for almost 10-15 minutes.
6. Serve and enjoy.

Tortellini With Spicy Dipping Sauce

Servings: 4
Cooking Time: 20 Minutes
Ingredients:
- ¾ cup mayonnaise
- 2 tablespoons mustard
- 1 egg
- ½ cup flour
- ½ teaspoon dried oregano
- 1½ cups bread crumbs
- 2 tablespoons olive oil
- 2 cups frozen cheese tortellini

Directions:
1. Preheat the air fryer to 380°F (193°C).
2. In a small bowl, combine the mayonnaise and mustard and mix well. Set aside.
3. In a shallow bowl, beat the egg. In a separate bowl, combine the flour and oregano. In another bowl, combine the bread crumbs and olive oil, and mix well.
4. Drop the tortellini, a few at a time, into the egg, then into the flour, then into the egg again, and then into the bread crumbs to coat. Put into the air fryer basket, cooking in batches.
5. Air fry for about 10 minutes, shaking halfway through the cooking time, or until the tortellini are crisp and golden brown on the outside. Serve with the mayonnaise mixture.

Enticing Pork Meatballs

Servings: 8
Cooking Time: 17 Minutes
Ingredients:
- 1 teaspoon cayenne pepper
- 2 teaspoons mustard
- 2 tablespoons Brie cheese, grated
- 5 garlic cloves, minced
- 2 small-sized yellow onions, peeled and chopped
- 1½ pounds ground pork
- Salt and black pepper, to taste

Directions:
1. Mix the cayenne pepper, mustard, grated Brie cheese, minced garlic, yellow onion, ground pork, salt, and pepper until everything is well incorporated.
2. Now, form the mixture into balls the size of golf a ball.
3. Cook for 17 minutes at 375 degrees F/ 190 degrees C.
4. Serve with your favorite sauce.

Poultry Recipes

Garlic Soy Chicken Thighs

Servings: 2
Cooking Time: 30 Minutes

Ingredients:
- 2 tablespoons chicken stock
- 2 tablespoons reduced-sodium soy sauce
- 1½ tablespoons sugar
- 4 garlic cloves, smashed and peeled
- 2 large scallions, cut into 2- to 3-inch batons, plus more, thinly sliced, for garnish
- 2 bone-in, skin-on chicken thighs (7 to 8 ounces / 198 to 227 g each)

Directions:
1. Preheat the air fryer to 375°F (191°C).
2. In a metal cake pan, combine the chicken stock, soy sauce, and sugar and stir until the sugar dissolves. Add the garlic cloves, scallions, and chicken thighs, turning the thighs to coat them in the marinade, then resting them skin-side up. Place the pan in the air fryer and bake, flipping the thighs every 5 minutes after the first 10 minutes, until the chicken is cooked through and the marinade is reduced to a sticky glaze over the chicken, about 30 minutes.
3. Remove the pan from the air fryer and serve the chicken thighs warm, with any remaining glaze spooned over top and sprinkled with more sliced scallions.

Za'atar Chicken Thighs

Servings: 4
Cooking Time: 35 Minutes

Ingredients:
- 4 chicken thighs
- 2 sprigs thyme
- 1 onion, cut into chunks
- 2 ½ tablespoons za'atar
- ½ teaspoon cinnamon
- 2 garlic cloves, smashed
- 1 lemon juice
- 1 lemon zest
- ¼ cup olive oil
- ¼ teaspoon black pepper
- 1 teaspoon salt

Directions:
1. Add oil, lemon juice, lemon zest, cinnamon, garlic, black pepper, 2 tablespoon za'atar, and salt in a large zip-lock bag and shake well.
2. Add chicken, thyme, and onion to bag and shake well to coat. Place in refrigerator for overnight.
3. At 380 degrees F/ 195 degrees C, preheat your air fryer.
4. Add marinated chicken in air fryer basket and cook at 380 degrees F/ 195 degrees C for 15 minutes.
5. Turn chicken to another side and sprinkle with remaining za'atar spice, then cook for 15-18 minutes more.
6. Serve and enjoy.

Greek Chicken Kebabs

Servings: 4
Cooking Time: 15 Minutes
Ingredients:

- 3 tablespoons freshly squeezed lemon juice
- 2 teaspoons olive oil
- 2 tablespoons chopped fresh flat-leaf parsley
- ½ teaspoon dried oregano
- ½ teaspoon dried mint
- 1 pound low-sodium boneless skinless chicken breasts, cut into 1-inch pieces
- 1 cup cherry tomatoes
- 1 small yellow summer squash, cut into 1-inch cubes

Directions:

1. In a large bowl, whisk the lemon juice, olive oil, parsley, oregano, and mint.
2. Add the chicken and stir to coat. Let stand for 10 minutes at room temperature.
3. Alternating the items, thread the chicken, tomatoes, and squash onto 8 bamboo (see Tip, here) or metal skewers that fit in an air fryer. Brush with marinade.
4. Grill the kebabs for about 15 minutes, brushing once with any remaining marinade, until the chicken reaches an internal temperature of 165°F on a meat thermometer. Discard any remaining marinade. Serve immediately.

Turkish Chicken Kebabs

Servings: 4
Cooking Time: 15 Minutes
Ingredients:

- ¼ cup plain Greek yogurt
- 1 tablespoon minced garlic
- 1 tablespoon tomato paste
- 1 tablespoon fresh lemon juice
- 1 tablespoon vegetable oil
- 1 teaspoon kosher salt
- 1 teaspoon ground cumin
- 1 teaspoon sweet Hungarian paprika
- ½ teaspoon ground cinnamon
- ½ teaspoon black pepper
- ½ teaspoon cayenne pepper
- 1 pound (454 g) boneless, skinless chicken thighs, quartered crosswise

Directions:

1. In a large bowl, combine the yogurt, garlic, tomato paste, lemon juice, vegetable oil, salt, cumin, paprika, cinnamon, black pepper, and cayenne. Stir until the spices are blended into the yogurt.
2. Add the chicken to the bowl and toss until well coated. Marinate at room temperature for 30 minutes, or cover and refrigerate for up to 24 hours.
3. Preheat the air fryer to 375°F (191°C).
4. Arrange the chicken in a single layer in the air fryer basket. Air fry for 10 minutes. Turn the chicken and air fry for 5 minutes more. Use a meat thermometer to ensure the chicken has reached an internal temperature of 165°F (74°C).
5. Serve warm.

Sweet And Sour Chicken Drumsticks

Servings: 6
Cooking Time: 40 Minutes

Ingredients:

- 6 chicken drumsticks
- 1 cup water
- ¼ cup tomato paste
- 1 cup soy sauce
- 1 cup white vinegar
- ¾ cup sugar
- ¾ cup minced onion
- ¼ cup minced garlic
- Black pepper and salt to taste

Directions:

1. Place all the recipe ingredients in a Ziploc bag and refrigerate for 2 hours in the fridge.
2. At 375 degrees F/ 190 degrees C, heat your Air Fryer in advance.
3. Set a suitable grill pan accessory in the air fryer.
4. Cook the chicken in the preheated air fryer for 40 minutes in total.
5. Turn chicken every 10 minutes for even grilling.
6. Meanwhile, pour the prepared marinade in a suitable saucepan and heat over medium flame until the sauce thickens.
7. Before serving the chicken, brush with the glaze.

Chicken Manchurian

Servings: 2
Cooking Time: 20 Minutes

Ingredients:

- 1 pound (454 g) boneless, skinless chicken breasts, cut into 1-inch pieces
- ¼ cup ketchup
- 1 tablespoon tomato-based chili sauce, such as Heinz
- 1 tablespoon soy sauce
- 1 tablespoon rice vinegar
- 2 teaspoons vegetable oil
- 1 teaspoon hot sauce, such as Tabasco
- ½ teaspoon garlic powder
- ¼ teaspoon cayenne pepper
- 2 scallions, thinly sliced
- Cooked white rice, for serving

Directions:

1. Preheat the air fryer to 350°F (177°C).
2. In a bowl, combine the chicken, ketchup, chili sauce, soy sauce, vinegar, oil, hot sauce, garlic powder, cayenne, and three-quarters of the scallions and toss until evenly coated.
3. Scrape the chicken and sauce into a metal cake pan and place the pan in the air fryer. Bake until the chicken is cooked through and the sauce is reduced to a thick glaze, about 20 minutes, flipping the chicken pieces halfway through.
4. Remove the pan from the air fryer. Spoon the chicken and sauce over rice and top with the remaining scallions. Serve immediately.

Mouthwatering Chicken Wings

Servings: 4
Cooking Time: 40 Minutes
Ingredients:
- 2 pounds' chicken wings
- ⅛ teaspoon paprika
- 2 teaspoons seasoned salt
- ½ cup coconut flour
- ¼ teaspoon garlic powder
- ¼ teaspoon chili powder

Directions:
1. At 370 degrees F/ 185 degrees C, preheat your air fryer.
2. In a suitable bowl, add all the recipe ingredients except chicken wings and mix well.
3. Add chicken wings into the bowl coat well.
4. Grease its air fryer basket with cooking spray.
5. Add chicken wings into the air fryer basket.
6. Cook for 35-40 minutes. Shake halfway through.
7. Serve and enjoy.

Chicken Satay

Servings:4
Cooking Time: 12 To 18 Minutes
Ingredients:
- ½ cup crunchy peanut butter
- ⅓ cup chicken broth
- 3 tablespoons low-sodium soy sauce
- 2 tablespoons lemon juice
- 2 cloves garlic, minced
- 2 tablespoons olive oil
- 1 teaspoon curry powder
- 1 pound chicken tenders

Directions:
1. In a medium bowl, combine the peanut butter, chicken broth, soy sauce, lemon juice, garlic, olive oil, and curry powder, and mix well with a wire whisk until smooth. Remove 2 tablespoons of this mixture to a small bowl. Put remaining sauce into a serving bowl and set aside.
2. Add the chicken tenders to the bowl with the 2 tablespoons sauce and stir to coat. Let stand for a few minutes to marinate, then run a bamboo skewer through each chicken tender lengthwise.
3. Put the chicken in the air fryer basket and cook in batches for 6 to 9 minutes or until the chicken reaches 165°F on a meat thermometer. Serve the chicken with the reserved sauce.

Chicken Burgers With Parmesan Cheese

Servings: 4
Cooking Time: 15 Minutes

Ingredients:

- 1 palmful dried basil
- ⅓ cup Parmesan cheese, grated
- 2 teaspoons dried marjoram
- ⅓ teaspoon ancho chili powder
- 2 teaspoons dried parsley flakes
- ½ teaspoon onion powder
- Toppings, to serve
- ⅓ teaspoon porcini powder
- 1 teaspoon salt flakes
- 1-pound chicken meat, ground
- 2 teaspoons cumin powder
- ⅓ teaspoon red pepper flakes, crushed
- 1 teaspoon freshly black pepper

Directions:

1. Generously grease an Air Fryer basket with a thin layer of vegetable oil.
2. In a mixing dish, combine chicken meat with all seasonings.
3. Shape into 4 patties and coat them with grated parmesan cheese.
4. Cook chicken burgers in the preheated Air Fryer for almost 15 minutes at 345 degrees F/ 175 degrees C, working in batches, flipping them once.
5. Serve with toppings of choice.

Buffalo Chicken Wings

Servings: 6
Cooking Time: 20 Minutes

Ingredients:

- 16 chicken drumettes (party wings)
- 1 teaspoon garlic powder
- Chicken seasoning or rub
- Pepper
- Cooking oil
- ¼ cup Frank's RedHot Buffalo Wings Sauce

Directions:

1. Season the drumettes with the garlic powder and chicken seasoning and pepper to taste.
2. Place the chicken in the air fryer. It is okay to stack the drumettes on top of each other. Spray them with cooking oil. Cook for 5 minutes.
3. Remove the basket and shake it to ensure all of the pieces will cook fully. Cook for an additional 5 minutes.
4. Open the air fryer and transfer the drumettes to a large bowl. Toss the drumettes with the Buffalo wing sauce, ensuring each is covered.
5. Return the drumettes to the air fryer. Cook for 7 minutes.
6. Cool before serving.

Chicken And Veggies Salad

Servings: 2
Cooking Time: 12 Minutes

Ingredients:

- ½ pound chicken breasts, boneless and skinless
- 1 cup grape tomatoes, halved
- 1 Serrano pepper, deveined and chopped
- 2 bell peppers, deveined and chopped
- 2 tablespoons olives, pitted and sliced
- 1 cucumber, sliced
- 1 red onion, sliced
- 1 cup arugula
- 1 cup baby spinach
- ¼ cup mayonnaise
- 2 tablespoons Greek-style yogurt
- 1 teaspoon lime juice
- ¼ teaspoon oregano
- ¼ teaspoon basil
- ¼ teaspoon red pepper flakes, crushed
- Sea salt, to taste
- Ground black pepper, to taste

Directions:

1. Before cooking, heat your air fryer to 380 degrees F/ 195 degrees C.
2. Using a nonstick cooking oil, spray the chicken breasts.
3. Transfer the chicken breasts inside the air fryer basket.
4. Cook in your air fryer for 12 minutes.
5. When the cooking time is up, cool for a while and cut into strips.
6. In a salad bowl, add the chicken strips and the remaining ingredients. Then place in your refrigerator.
7. When ready, serve and enjoy!

Barbecued Chicken Skewers

Servings: 4
Cooking Time: 15 Minutes

Ingredients:

- 4 cloves garlic, chopped
- 4 scallions, chopped
- 2 tablespoons sesame seeds, toasted
- 1 tablespoon fresh ginger, grated
- ½ cup pineapple juice
- ½ cup soy sauce
- ⅓ cup sesame oil
- A pinch of black pepper

Directions:

1. Skew the tenders with any excess fat: trimmed.
2. In a bowl, mix the chopped garlic, scallions, sesame seeds, fresh ginger, the pineapple juice, soy sauce, sesame oil, and black pepper. Add the chicken skewers together with the mixture in the bowl and refrigerate for about 4 hours.
3. Before cooking, heat your air fryer to 375 degrees F/ 190 degrees C.
4. Cook the chicken skewers in the preheated air fryer for 12 minutes.

Southern Fried Chicken

Servings: 2
Cooking Time: 30 Minutes

Ingredients:
- 2 x 6-oz. boneless skinless chicken breasts
- 2 tbsp. hot sauce
- ½ tsp. onion powder
- 1 tbsp. chili powder
- 2 oz. pork rinds, finely ground

Directions:
1. Lengthwise cut the chicken breasts in half and rub in the hot sauce. Combine the onion powder with the chili powder, then rub into the chicken. Leave to marinate for at least a half hour.
2. Use the ground pork rinds to coat the chicken breasts in the ground pork rinds, covering them thoroughly. Place the chicken in your air fryer.
3. Set the fryer at 350 degrees F/ 175 degrees C and cook the chicken for 13 minutes. Flip the chicken and then cook the other side for another 13 minutes or until golden.
4. Test the chicken with a meat thermometer. When fully cooked, it should reach 165 degrees F/ 75 degrees C. Serve hot, with the sides of your choice.

Seasoned Chicken Thighs With Italian Herbs

Servings: 4
Cooking Time: 20 Minutes

Ingredients:
- 4 skin-on bone-in chicken thighs
- 2 tablespoons unsalted butter, melted
- 3 teaspoons Italian herbs
- ½ teaspoon garlic powder
- ¼ teaspoon onion powder

Directions:
1. Using a brush, coat the chicken thighs with the melted butter.
2. Combine the herbs with the garlic powder and onion powder, then massage into the chicken thighs.
3. Place the thighs your air fryer's basket.
4. Cook at almost exactly 380 degrees F/ 195 degrees C for 20 minutes, turning the chicken halfway through to cook on the other side.
5. Once the inner temperature has reached 165 degrees F/ 75 degrees C, remove from the fryer and serve.

Sweet-and-sour Drumsticks

Servings: 4
Cooking Time: 23 To 25 Minutes

Ingredients:

- 6 chicken drumsticks
- 3 tablespoons lemon juice, divided
- 3 tablespoons low-sodium soy sauce, divided
- 1 tablespoon peanut oil
- 3 tablespoons honey
- 3 tablespoons brown sugar
- 2 tablespoons ketchup
- ¼ cup pineapple juice

Directions:

1. Preheat the air fryer to 350°F (177°C).
2. Sprinkle the drumsticks with 1 tablespoon of lemon juice and 1 tablespoon of soy sauce. Place in the air fryer basket and drizzle with the peanut oil. Toss to coat. Bake for 18 minutes or until the chicken is almost done.
3. Meanwhile, in a metal bowl, combine the remaining 2 tablespoons of lemon juice, the remaining 2 tablespoons of soy sauce, honey, brown sugar, ketchup, and pineapple juice.
4. Add the cooked chicken to the bowl and stir to coat the chicken well with the sauce.
5. Place the metal bowl in the basket. Bake for 5 to 7 minutes or until the chicken is glazed and registers 165°F (74°C) on a meat thermometer. Serve warm.

Crispy Chicken Strips

Servings: 4
Cooking Time: 20 Minutes

Ingredients:

- 1 tablespoon olive oil
- 1 pound (454 g) boneless, skinless chicken tenderloins
- 1 teaspoon salt
- ½ teaspoon freshly ground black pepper
- ½ teaspoon paprika
- ½ teaspoon garlic powder
- ½ cup whole-wheat seasoned bread crumbs
- 1 teaspoon dried parsley
- Cooking spray

Directions:

1. Preheat the air fryer to 370°F (188°C). Spray the air fryer basket lightly with cooking spray.
2. In a medium bowl, toss the chicken with the salt, pepper, paprika, and garlic powder until evenly coated.
3. Add the olive oil and toss to coat the chicken evenly.
4. In a separate, shallow bowl, mix together the bread crumbs and parsley.
5. Coat each piece of chicken evenly in the bread crumb mixture.
6. Place the chicken in the air fryer basket in a single layer and spray it lightly with cooking spray. You may need to cook them in batches.
7. Air fry for 10 minutes. Flip the chicken over, lightly spray it with cooking spray, and air fry for an additional 8 to 10 minutes, until golden brown. Serve.

Teriyaki Chicken Bowls

Servings: 4
Cooking Time: 15 Minutes

Ingredients:

- Olive oil
- ⅓ cup soy sauce
- ⅓ cup honey
- 3 tablespoons white vinegar
- 1½ teaspoons dried thyme
- 1½ teaspoons paprika
- 1 teaspoon ground black pepper
- ½ teaspoon cayenne pepper
- ½ teaspoon ground allspice
- 1 pound boneless, skinless chicken tenderloins
- 2 cups cooked brown rice
- 2 cups steamed broccoli florets

Directions:

1. Spray a fryer basket lightly with olive oil.
2. In a large bowl, mix together the soy sauce, honey, white vinegar, thyme, paprika, black pepper, cayenne pepper, and allspice to make a marinade.
3. Add the tenderloins to the marinade and stir to coat. Cover and refrigerate for 30 minutes.
4. Place the chicken in the fryer basket in a single layer. You may need to cook the chicken in batches. Reserve the marinade.
5. Air fry for 6 minutes. Turn the chicken over and brush with some of the remaining marinade. Cook until chicken reaches an internal temperature of at least 165°F, an additional 5 to 7 minutes.
6. To assemble the bowls, place ½ cup of brown rice, ½ cup of steamed broccoli, and 2 chicken tenderloins into each bowl and serve.

Spice Chicken With Broccoli

Servings: 4
Cooking Time: 20 Minutes

Ingredients:

- 1-pound chicken breast, boneless, and cut into chunks
- 2 cups broccoli florets
- 2 teaspoons hot sauce
- 2 teaspoons vinegar
- 1 teaspoon sesame oil
- 1 tablespoon soy sauce
- 1 tablespoon ginger, minced
- ½ teaspoon garlic powder
- 1 tablespoon olive oil
- ½ onion, sliced
- Black pepper
- Salt

Directions:

1. Add all the recipe ingredients into the suitable mixing bowl and toss well.
2. Grease its air fryer basket with cooking spray.
3. Transfer chicken and broccoli mixture into the air fryer basket.
4. Cook at almost 380 degrees F/ 195 degrees C for almost 15-20 minutes. Shake halfway through.
5. Serve and enjoy.

Mayo Turkey Breasts

Servings: 4
Cooking Time: 60 Minutes

Ingredients:

- 3 pounds' boneless turkey breast
- ¼ cup mayonnaise
- 2 teaspoons poultry seasoning
- Black pepper and salt to taste
- ½ teaspoon garlic powder

Directions:

1. At 360 degrees F/ 180 degrees C, preheat your air fryer. Season the turkey with mayonnaise, seasoning, salt, garlic powder, and black pepper.
2. Cook the turkey in the preheated Air Fryer for 1 hour at 360 degrees F/ 180 degrees C.
3. Turning after every 15 minutes.
4. Serve.

Tasty Pasta Chicken

Servings: 4
Cooking Time: 15 Minutes

Ingredients:

- ¼ cup green onions, chopped
- 1 green garlic, minced
- 4 tablespoons seasoned breadcrumbs
- ½ teaspoon cumin powder
- 1 cup chicken meat, ground
- 1 sweet red pepper, minced
- ¼ teaspoon mixed peppercorns, ground
- 1 package penne pasta, cooked
- 1 tablespoon coriander, minced
- ½ teaspoon sea salt

Directions:

1. Mix thoroughly red pepper, garlic, green onions, and the chicken in a medium sized bowl.
2. Mix in seasonings and the breadcrumbs until well combined.
3. Make small balls out from the mixture.
4. On a flat kitchen surface, plug your air fryer and turn it on.
5. Before cooking, heat your air fryer to 350 degrees F/ 175 degrees C for about 4 to 5 minutes.
6. Gently coat an air fryer basket with cooking oil or spray.
7. Arrange the balls to the greased basket.
8. When cooked, remove the balls from the air fryer and serve warm with cooked pasta as you like.

Roasted Chicken And Vegetable Salad

Servings: 4
Cooking Time: 10 To 13 Minutes

Ingredients:

- 3 (4-ounce / 113-g) low-sodium boneless, skinless chicken breasts, cut into 1-inch cubes
- 1 small red onion, sliced
- 1 red bell pepper, sliced
- 1 cup green beans, cut into 1-inch pieces
- 2 tablespoons low-fat ranch salad dressing
- 2 tablespoons freshly squeezed lemon juice
- ½ teaspoon dried basil
- 4 cups mixed lettuce

Directions:

1. Preheat the air fryer to 400°F (204°C).
2. In the air fryer basket, roast the chicken, red onion, red bell pepper, and green beans for 10 to 13 minutes, or until the chicken reaches an internal temperature of 165°F (74°C) on a meat thermometer, tossing the food in the basket once during cooking.
3. While the chicken cooks, in a serving bowl, mix the ranch dressing, lemon juice, and basil.
4. Transfer the chicken and vegetables to a serving bowl and toss with the dressing to coat. Serve immediately on lettuce leaves.

Marinated Chicken With Peppercorns

Servings: 4
Cooking Time: 15 Minutes

Ingredients:

- 1 ½ cups all-purpose flour
- Salt, as needed
- ½ teaspoon peppercorns, cracked
- 1 teaspoon shallot powder
- ¾ cup of buttermilk
- 1 pound chicken tenders
- ½ teaspoon cumin powder
- 1 tablespoon sesame oil
- 1 ½ teaspoon smoked cayenne pepper

Directions:

1. In a deep marinade dish, add chicken and the buttermilk and stir gently to coat well. Marinate the chicken for 1 hour.
2. Mix thoroughly all seasonings with the flour in a medium sized bowl.
3. Dredge the chicken in the seasoning-flour mixture and coat well.
4. Then add in the buttermilk and put in the flour mixture to coat.
5. Using sesame oil, grease the chicken.
6. On a flat kitchen surface, plug your air fryer and turn it on.
7. Before cooking, heat your air fryer to 365 degrees F/ 185 degrees C for about 4 to 5 minutes.
8. Spread the chicken tenders in the air fryer basket and insert the basket inside your air fryer.
9. Cook for 15 minutes.
10. During cooking, shake the basket every 5 minutes.
11. When cooked, remove from the air fryer and serve warm.

Beef, Pork & Lamb Recipes

Pork And Ginger Meatball Bowl

Servings: 4
Cooking Time: 15 Minutes

Ingredients:

- Olive oil
- 2 pounds lean ground pork
- 2 eggs, beaten
- 1 cup whole-wheat panko bread crumbs
- 1 green onion, thinly sliced
- 2 teaspoons soy sauce
- 2 teaspoons minced garlic
- ½ teaspoon ground ginger
- 2 cups cooked rice noodles (cooked according to package directions)
- 1 cup peeled and shredded carrots
- 1 cup peeled and thinly sliced cucumber
- 1 cup light Asian sesame dressing

Directions:

1. Spray a fryer basket lightly with olive oil.
2. In a large bowl, mix together the pork, eggs, bread crumbs, green onion, soy sauce, garlic, and ginger.
3. Using a small cookie scoop, form 24 meatballs.
4. Place the meatballs in a single layer in the fryer basket. Lightly spray meatballs with olive oil. You may need to cook the meatballs in batches.
5. Air fry until the meatballs reach an internal temperature of at least 145°F, 10 to 15 minutes, shaking the basket every 5 minutes for even cooking.
6. To assemble the bowls, place ½ cup rice noodles, ¼ cup carrots, and ¼ cup cucumber in 4 bowls. Drizzle each bowl with ¼ cup sesame dressing and top with 6 meatballs.

Beef And Cheddar Burgers

Servings: 4
Cooking Time: 25 Minutes

Ingredients:

- 1 tablespoon olive oil
- 1 onion, sliced into rings
- 1 teaspoon garlic, minced or puréed
- 1 teaspoon mustard
- 1 teaspoon basil
- 1 teaspoon mixed herbs
- Salt and ground black pepper, to taste
- 1 teaspoon tomato, puréed
- 4 buns
- 1 ounce (28 g) Cheddar cheese, sliced
- 10.5 ounces (298 g) beef, minced
- Salad leaves

Directions:

1. Preheat the air fryer to 390ºF (199ºC).
2. Grease the air fryer with olive oil and allow it to warm up.
3. Put the diced onion in the air fryer and air fry until they turn golden brown.
4. Mix in the garlic, mustard, basil, herbs, salt, and pepper, and air fry for 25 minutes.
5. Lay 2 to 3 onion rings and puréed tomato on two of the buns. Put one slice of cheese and the layer of beef on top. Top with salad leaves before closing off the sandwich with the other buns.
6. Serve immediately.

Avocado Buttered Flank Steak

Servings: 1
Cooking Time: 12 Minutes

Ingredients:
- 1 flank steak
- Salt and ground black pepper, to taste
- 2 avocados
- 2 tablespoons butter, melted
- ½ cup chimichurri sauce

Directions:
1. Rub the flank steak with salt and pepper to taste and leave to sit for 20 minutes.
2. Preheat the air fryer to 400°F (204°C) and place a rack inside.
3. Halve the avocados and take out the pits. Spoon the flesh into a bowl and mash with a fork. Mix in the melted butter and chimichurri sauce, making sure everything is well combined.
4. Put the steak in the air fryer and air fry for 6 minutes. Flip over and allow to air fry for another 6 minutes.
5. Serve the steak with the avocado butter.

Parmesan Sausage Meatballs

Servings: 8
Cooking Time: 15 Minutes

Ingredients:
- 1 pound Italian sausage
- 1-pound ground beef
- ½ teaspoon Italian seasoning
- ½ teaspoon red pepper flakes
- 1 ½ cups Parmesan cheese, grated
- 2 egg, lightly beaten
- 2 tablespoons parsley, chopped
- 2 garlic cloves, minced
- ¼ cup onion, minced
- Black pepper
- Salt

Directions:
1. Add all the recipe ingredients into the suitable mixing bowl and mix until well combined.
2. Grease its air fryer basket with cooking spray.
3. Make meatballs from bowl mixture and place into the air fryer basket.
4. Cook at almost 350 degrees F/ 175 degrees C for almost 15 minutes.
5. Serve and enjoy.

Sweet-and-sour Polish Sausage

Servings: 4
Cooking Time: 10 To 15 Minutes

Ingredients:

- ¾ pound Polish sausage
- 1 red bell pepper, cut into 1-inch strips
- ½ cup minced onion
- 3 tablespoons brown sugar
- ⅓ cup ketchup
- 2 tablespoons mustard
- 2 tablespoons apple cider vinegar
- ½ cup chicken broth

Directions:

1. Cut the sausage into 1½-inch pieces and put into a 6-inch metal bowl. Add the pepper and minced onion.
2. In a small bowl, combine the brown sugar, ketchup, mustard, apple cider vinegar, and chicken broth, and mix well. Pour into the bowl.
3. Roast for 10 to 15 minutes or until the sausage is hot, the vegetables tender, and the sauce bubbling and slightly thickened.
4. Did You Know? Polish sausage is almost always fully cooked when it is sold; read the label carefully to make sure you buy a fully cooked type for this recipe. Uncooked sausages are too fatty and release too much grease to cook in this appliance.

Sweet And Spicy Pork Chops

Servings: 4
Cooking Time: 15 Minutes

Ingredients:

- 1 tablespoon olive oil, plus more for spraying
- 3 tablespoons brown sugar
- ½ teaspoon cayenne pepper
- ½ teaspoon garlic powder
- ½ teaspoon salt
- ¼ teaspoon freshly ground black pepper
- 4 thin boneless pork chops, trimmed of excess fat

Directions:

1. Spray a fryer basket lightly with olive oil.
2. In a small bowl, mix together the brown sugar, 1 tablespoon of olive oil, cayenne pepper, garlic powder, salt, and black pepper.
3. Coat each pork chop with the marinade, shaking them to remove any excess, and place in the fryer basket in a single layer. You may need to cook them in batches.
4. Air fry for 7 minutes. Flip the pork chops over and brush with more marinade. Cook until the chops reach an internal temperature of 145°F, an additional 5 to 8 minutes.

Citrus Pork Loin Roast

Servings: 8
Cooking Time: 45 Minutes

Ingredients:
- 1 tablespoon lime juice
- 1 tablespoon orange marmalade
- 1 teaspoon coarse brown mustard
- 1 teaspoon curry powder
- 1 teaspoon dried lemongrass
- 2 pound (907 g) boneless pork loin roast
- Salt and ground black pepper, to taste
- Cooking spray

Directions:
1. Preheat the air fryer to 360°F (182°C).
2. Mix the lime juice, marmalade, mustard, curry powder, and lemongrass.
3. Rub mixture all over the surface of the pork loin. Season with salt and pepper.
4. Spray air fryer basket with cooking spray and place pork roast diagonally in the basket.
5. Air fry for approximately 45 minutes, until the internal temperature reaches at least 145°F (63°C).
6. Wrap roast in foil and let rest for 10 minutes before slicing.
7. Serve immediately.

Tomato Pork Burgers

Servings: 4
Cooking Time: 7 Minutes

Ingredients:
- ½ cup Greek yogurt
- 2 tablespoons mustard, divided
- 1 tablespoon lemon juice
- ¼ cup sliced red cabbage
- ¼ cup grated carrots
- 1-pound lean ground pork
- ½ teaspoon paprika
- 1 cup mixed baby lettuce greens
- 2 small tomatoes, sliced
- 8 small whole-wheat sandwich buns, cut in ½

Directions:
1. In a suitable bowl, combine the yogurt, 1 tablespoon mustard, lemon juice, cabbage, and carrots; mix and refrigerate.
2. In a suitable bowl, combine the pork, remaining 1 tablespoon mustard, and paprika. Form into 8 small patties.
3. Set the sliders into the air fryer basket and cook for 7 minutes.
4. Make the burgers by placing adding the lettuce greens on a bun.
5. Top it with a tomato slice, the burgers, and the cabbage mixture.
6. Add the bun top and serve immediately.

Bbq Pork Chops With Vegetables

Servings: 5-6
Cooking Time: 20 Minutes

Ingredients:

- 6 pork chops
- 1 teaspoon onion powder
- ½ teaspoon garlic powder
- Ground black pepper and salt as needed
- ½ teaspoon cayenne pepper
- 1 teaspoon brown sugar
- ⅓ cup all-purpose flour

Directions:

1. To marinate, prepare a Ziploc bag, add the ingredients, seal and shake well.
2. Coat the cooking basket of your air fryer with cooking oil or spray.
3. Place the chops on the basket and then arrange the basket to the air fryer.
4. Cook the chops at 375 degrees F/ 190 degrees C for 20 minutes.
5. When done, serve warm with sautéed vegetables!

Cheese Ground Pork

Servings: 4
Cooking Time: 40 Minutes

Ingredients:

- 1 tablespoon olive oil
- 1 ½ pounds pork, ground
- Salt and black pepper, to taste
- 1 medium-sized leek, sliced
- 1 teaspoon fresh garlic, minced
- 2 carrots, trimmed and sliced
- 1 (2-ounce) jar pimiento, drained and chopped
- 1 can (10 ¾-ounces) condensed cream of mushroom soup
- 1 cup water
- ½ cup ale
- 1 cup cream cheese
- ½ cup soft fresh breadcrumbs
- 1 tablespoon fresh cilantro, chopped

Directions:

1. At 320 degrees F/ 160 degrees C, preheat your Air Fryer.
2. Spread the olive oil in a suitable baking dish and heat for 1 to 2 minutes.
3. Add the pork, salt, black pepper and cook for 6 minutes, crumbling with a fork.
4. Then stir in the leeks and cook for 4 to 5 minutes, with occasional stirring.
5. Add the garlic, carrots, pimiento, mushroom soup, water, ale, and cream cheese.
6. Gently stir to combine.
7. Turn the temperature to 370 degrees F/ 185 degrees C.
8. Top with the breadcrumbs.
9. Place the stuffed baking dish in the cooking basket and cook approximately 30 minutes or until everything is thoroughly cooked.
10. Serve garnished with fresh cilantro.

Beef And Vegetable Cubes

Servings: 4
Cooking Time: 17 Minutes

Ingredients:

- 2 tablespoons olive oil
- 1 tablespoon apple cider vinegar
- 1 teaspoon fine sea salt
- ½ teaspoons ground black pepper
- 1 teaspoon shallot powder
- ¾ teaspoon smoked cayenne pepper
- ½ teaspoons garlic powder
- ¼ teaspoon ground cumin
- 1 pound (454 g) top round steak, cut into cubes
- 4 ounces (113 g) broccoli, cut into florets
- 4 ounces (113 g) mushrooms, sliced
- 1 teaspoon dried basil
- 1 teaspoon celery seeds

Directions:

1. Massage the olive oil, vinegar, salt, black pepper, shallot powder, cayenne pepper, garlic powder, and cumin into the cubed steak, ensuring to coat each piece evenly.
2. Allow to marinate for a minimum of 3 hours.
3. Preheat the air fryer to 365°F (185°C).
4. Put the beef cubes in the air fryer basket and air fry for 12 minutes.
5. When the steak is cooked through, place it in a bowl.
6. Wipe the grease from the basket and pour in the vegetables. Season them with basil and celery seeds.
7. Increase the temperature of the air fryer to 400°F (204°C) and air fry for 5 to 6 minutes. When the vegetables are hot, serve them with the steak.

Steak Fingers

Servings: 4
Cooking Time: 15 Minutes

Ingredients:

- Olive oil
- ½ cup whole-wheat flour
- 1 teaspoon seasoned salt
- ½ teaspoon freshly ground black pepper
- ¼ teaspoon cayenne pepper
- 2 eggs, beaten
- ½ cup low-fat milk
- 1 pound cube steaks, cut into 1-inch-wide strips

Directions:

1. Spray a fryer basket lightly with olive oil.
2. In a shallow bowl, mix together the flour, salt, black pepper, and cayenne.
3. In another shallow bowl, whisk together the eggs and milk.
4. Dredge the steak strips in the flour mixture, coat with the egg mixture, and dredge in the flour mixture once more to coat completely.
5. Place the steak strips in the fryer basket in a single layer and spray lightly with olive oil. You may need to cook the steak in batches.
6. Air fry for 8 minutes. Flip the steak strips over and lightly spray with olive oil. Cook until golden brown and crispy, an additional 4 to 7 minutes.

Cheesy Beef Meatballs

Servings: 6
Cooking Time: 18 Minutes

Ingredients:
- 1 pound (454 g) ground beef
- ½ cup grated Parmesan cheese
- 1 tablespoon minced garlic
- ½ cup Mozzarella cheese
- 1 teaspoon freshly ground pepper

Directions:
1. Preheat the air fryer to 400°F (204°C).
2. In a bowl, mix all the ingredients together.
3. Roll the meat mixture into 5 generous meatballs.
4. Air fry inside the air fryer at 165°F (74°C) for about 18 minutes.
5. Serve immediately.

Beer Corned Beef

Servings: 3
Cooking Time: 50 Minutes

Ingredients:
- 1 whole onion, chopped
- 4 carrots, chopped
- 12 oz. bottle beer
- 1½ cups chicken broth
- 4 pounds corned beef

Directions:
1. At 380 degrees F/ 195 degrees C, preheat your air fryer.
2. Cover beef with beer and set aside for 20 minutes.
3. Place carrots, onion and beef in a pot and heat over high heat.
4. Add in broth and bring to a boil. Drain the meat and veggies.
5. Top with beef spice.
6. Place the meat and veggies in air fryer's cooking basket and cook for 30 minutes.
7. Serve.

Glazed Tender Pork Chops

Servings: 3
Cooking Time: 14 Minutes
Ingredients:
- 3 pork chops, rinsed and pat dry
- ¼ teaspoon smoked paprika
- ½ teaspoon garlic powder
- 2 teaspoons olive oil
- Black pepper
- Salt

Directions:
1. Coat pork chops with paprika, olive oil, garlic powder, black pepper, and salt.
2. Place the prepared pork chops in air fryer basket and cook at almost 380 degrees F/ 195 degrees C for almost 10-14 minutes. Turn halfway through the cooking time.
3. Serve and enjoy.

Garlic Pork Roast

Servings: 8
Cooking Time: 30 Minutes
Ingredients:
- 2 lbs. pork roast
- 1 ½-teaspoon garlic powder
- 1 ½-teaspoon coriander powder
- ⅓-teaspoon salt
- 1 ½-teaspoon black pepper
- 1 ½ dried thyme
- 1 ½-teaspoon dried oregano
- 1 ½-teaspoon cumin powder
- 3 cups water
- 1 lemon, halved

Directions:
1. Mix up the garlic powder, coriander powder, salt, black pepper, thyme, oregano and cumin powder in a suitable bowl.
2. Dry the pork well and then poke holes all around it using a fork.
3. Smear the oregano rub thoroughly on all sides with your hands and squeeze the lemon juice all over it. Set aside for 5 minutes.
4. Cook the pork at 300 degrees F/ 150 degrees C for 10 minutes.
5. Turn the pork and increase the temperature to 350 F and continue cooking for 10 minutes.
6. Once ready, remove it and place it in on a chopping board to sit for 4 minutes before slicing. Serve the pork slices with a side of sautéed asparagus and hot sauce.

Unique Beef Cheeseburgers

Servings: 4

Cooking Time: 15 Minutes

Ingredients:

- ½ lb. ground beef
- ⅓ cup breadcrumbs
- 2 tablespoons parsley, finely chopped
- 3 tablespoons parmesan cheese, shredded
- ½ teaspoon salt
- ⅓ teaspoon pepper
- 4 slices Cheddar cheese
- 4 burger buns
- 1 red onion, sliced
- 4 romaine lettuce leaves
- 4 teaspoons mayonnaise
- 1cup pickles, sliced

Directions:

1. Mix the ground beef with breadcrumbs, parmesan cheese, parsley, salt and pepper well in a suitable dish.
2. Form 4 patties from the meat mixture.
3. Cook the patties in your air fryer at 390 degrees F/ 200 degrees C for 13 minutes.
4. After that, place the cheese slices on the top and cook for 1 minute more.
5. When cooked, top with pickles, red onion, lettuce leaves, and mayonnaise.
6. Enjoy!

Pork Tenderloin With Apple Juice

Servings: 4

Cooking Time: 19 Minutes

Ingredients:

- 1 1-pound pork tenderloin, cut into 4 pieces
- 1 tablespoon apple butter
- 2 teaspoons olive oil
- 2 Granny Smith apples, sliced
- 3 celery stalks, sliced
- 1 onion, sliced
- ½ teaspoon dried marjoram
- ⅓ cup apple juice

Directions:

1. Rub each piece of pork with the apple butter and olive oil.
2. In a medium metal bowl, mix the pork, apples, celery, onion, marjoram, and apple juice.
3. Set the bowl into the air fryer and roast for 14 to 19 minutes.
4. Stir once during cooking.
5. Serve immediately.

Lollipop Lamb Chops

Servings: 4
Cooking Time: 7 Minutes

Ingredients:

- ½ small clove garlic
- ¼ cup packed fresh parsley
- ¾ cup packed fresh mint
- ½ teaspoon lemon juice
- ¼ cup grated Parmesan cheese
- ⅓ cup shelled pistachios
- ¼ teaspoon salt
- ½ cup olive oil
- 8 lamb chops (1 rack)
- 2 tablespoons vegetable oil
- Salt and freshly ground black pepper, to taste
- 1 tablespoon dried rosemary, chopped
- 1 tablespoon dried thyme

Directions:

1. Make the pesto by combining the garlic, parsley and mint in a food processor and process until finely chopped. Add the lemon juice, Parmesan cheese, pistachios and salt. Process until all the ingredients have turned into a paste. With the processor running, slowly pour the olive oil in. Scrape the sides of the processor with a spatula and process for another 30 seconds.
2. Preheat the air fryer to 400°F (204°C).
3. Rub both sides of the lamb chops with vegetable oil and season with salt, pepper, rosemary and thyme, pressing the herbs into the meat gently with the fingers. Transfer the lamb chops to the air fryer basket.
4. Air fry the lamb chops for 5 minutes. Flip the chops over and air fry for an additional 2 minutes.
5. Serve the lamb chops with mint pesto drizzled on top.

Roasted Pork Tenderloin

Servings: 6
Cooking Time: 1 Hour

Ingredients:

- 1 (3-pound) pork tenderloin
- 2 tablespoons extra-virgin olive oil
- 2 garlic cloves, minced
- 1 teaspoon dried basil
- 1 teaspoon dried oregano
- 1 teaspoon dried thyme
- Salt
- Pepper

Directions:

1. Drizzle the pork tenderloin with the olive oil.
2. Rub the garlic, basil, oregano, thyme, and salt and pepper to taste all over the tenderloin.
3. Place the tenderloin in the air fryer. Cook for 45 minutes.
4. Use a meat thermometer to test for doneness. (See Cooking tip.)
5. Open the air fryer and flip the pork tenderloin. Cook for an additional 15 minutes.
6. Remove the cooked pork from the air fryer and allow it to rest for 10 minutes before cutting.

Rosemary Lamb Chops

Servings: 4
Cooking Time: 15 Minutes
Ingredients:
- 8 (3-ounce) lamb chops
- 2 teaspoons extra-virgin olive oil
- 1½ teaspoons chopped fresh rosemary
- 1 garlic clove, minced
- Salt
- Pepper

Directions:
1. Drizzle the lamb chops with olive oil.
2. In a small bowl, combine the rosemary, garlic, and salt and pepper to taste. Rub the seasoning onto the front and back of each lamb chop.
3. Place the lamb chops in the air fryer. It is okay to stack them. Cook for 10 minutes.
4. Open the air fryer. Flip the lamb chops. Cook for an additional 5 minutes.
5. Cool before serving.

Jerk Pork Butt Pieces

Servings: 4
Cooking Time: 20 Minutes
Ingredients:
- 1 ½ pounds pork butt, chopped into pieces
- 3 tablespoons jerk paste

Directions:
1. Add meat and jerk paste into the bowl and coat well. Place in the fridge for overnight.
2. Grease its air fryer basket with cooking spray.
3. At 390 degrees F/ 200 degrees C, preheat your air fryer.
4. Add marinated meat into the air fryer and cook for 20 minutes. Turn halfway through the cooking time.
5. Serve and enjoy.

Fish And Seafood Recipes

Tuna Veggie Stir-fry

Servings: 4
Cooking Time: 7 To 12 Minutes

Ingredients:
- 1 tablespoon olive oil
- 1 red bell pepper, chopped
- 1 cup green beans, cut into 2-inch pieces
- 1 onion, sliced
- 2 cloves garlic, sliced
- 2 tablespoons low-sodium soy sauce
- 1 tablespoon honey
- ½ pound fresh tuna, cubed

Directions:
1. In a 6-inch metal bowl, combine the olive oil, pepper, green beans, onion, and garlic.
2. Cook in the air fryer for 4 to 6 minutes, stirring once, until crisp and tender. Add soy sauce, honey, and tuna, and stir.
3. Cook for another 3 to 6 minutes, stirring once, until the tuna is cooked as desired. Tuna can be served rare or medium-rare, or you can cook it until well done.

Old Bay Shrimp

Servings: 6
Cooking Time: 5 Minutes

Ingredients:
- 1 ¼-pound/16-20 tiger shrimp
- 1 tablespoon olive oil
- ½ teaspoon old Bay seasoning
- ¼ teaspoon smoked paprika
- ¼ teaspoon black pepper

Directions:
1. At 390 degrees F/ 200 degrees C, preheat your air fryer.
2. Cover the shrimp using the oil and spices.
3. Spread the spiced shrimp in the air fryer basket and set the timer for 5 minutes.
4. Serve with your favorite side dish.

Crispy Herbed Salmon

Servings: 4
Cooking Time: 9 To 12 Minutes
Ingredients:
- 4 (6-ounce) skinless salmon fillets
- 3 tablespoons honey mustard
- ½ teaspoon dried thyme
- ½ teaspoon dried basil
- ¼ cup panko bread crumbs
- ⅓ cup crushed potato chips
- 2 tablespoons olive oil

Directions:
1. Place the salmon on a plate. In a small bowl, combine the mustard, thyme, and basil, and spread evenly over the salmon.
2. In another small bowl, combine the bread crumbs and potato chips and mix well. Drizzle in the olive oil and mix until combined.
3. Place the salmon in the air fryer basket and gently but firmly press the bread crumb mixture onto the top of each fillet.
4. Bake for 9 to 12 minutes or until the salmon reaches at least 145°F on a meat thermometer and the topping is browned and crisp.

Easy Air Fried Salmon

Servings: 2
Cooking Time: 10 Minutes
Ingredients:
- 2 salmon fillets, skinless and boneless
- 1 teaspoon olive oil
- Black pepper
- Salt

Directions:
1. Coat boneless salmon fillets with olive oil and season with black pepper and salt.
2. Place salmon fillets in air fryer basket and Cook at almost 360 degrees F/ 180 degrees C for 8-10 minutes.
3. Serve and enjoy.

Mustard-crusted Fish Fillets

Servings: 4
Cooking Time: 8 To 11 Minutes

Ingredients:
- 5 teaspoons low-sodium yellow mustard (see Tip)
- 1 tablespoon freshly squeezed lemon juice
- 4 (3.5-ounce) sole fillets
- ½ teaspoon dried thyme
- ½ teaspoon dried marjoram
- ⅛ teaspoon freshly ground black pepper
- 1 slice low-sodium whole-wheat bread, crumbled
- 2 teaspoons olive oil

Directions:
1. In a small bowl, mix the mustard and lemon juice. Spread this evenly over the fillets. Place them in the air fryer basket.
2. In another small bowl, mix the thyme, marjoram, pepper, bread crumbs, and olive oil. Mix until combined.
3. Gently but firmly press the spice mixture onto the top of each fish fillet.
4. Bake for 8 to 11 minutes, or until the fish reaches an internal temperature of at least 145°F on a meat thermometer and the topping is browned and crisp. Serve immediately.

Cajun Fish Tacos

Servings: 6
Cooking Time: 15 Minutes

Ingredients:
- 2 teaspoons avocado oil
- 1 tablespoon Cajun seasoning
- 4 (5 to 6 ounce) tilapia fillets
- 1 (14-ounce) package coleslaw mix
- 12 corn tortillas
- 2 limes, cut into wedges

Directions:
1. Line a fryer basket with a perforated air fryer liner.
2. In a medium, shallow bowl mix together the avocado oil and the Cajun seasoning to make a marinade. Add the tilapia fillets and coat evenly.
3. Place the fillets in the basket in a single layer, leaving room between each fillet. You may need to cook in batches.
4. Air fry until the fish is cooked and easily flakes with a fork, 10 to 15 minutes.
5. Assemble the tacos by placing some of the coleslaw mix in each tortilla. Add ⅓ of a tilapia fillet to each tortilla. Squeeze some lime juice over the top of each taco and serve.

Lime Cajun Shrimp

Servings: 4
Cooking Time: 8 Minutes

Ingredients:

- 1 pound shrimp, peeled and deveined
- 1 lime, cut into wedges
- ½ tablespoon chipotle chili in adobo, minced
- 1 tablespoon Cajun seasoning
- 2 tablespoons olive oil
- Black pepper
- Salt

Directions:

1. Add all the recipe ingredients into the suitable bowl and toss well to coat. Place in the fridge for 1 hour.
2. Grease its air fryer basket with cooking spray.
3. Add marinated shrimp into the air fryer basket and cook at almost 400 degrees F/ 205 degrees C for 8 minutes.
4. Serve and enjoy.

Healthy Salmon With Cardamom

Servings: 2
Cooking Time: 12 Minutes

Ingredients:

- 2 salmon fillets
- 1 tablespoon olive oil
- ¼ teaspoon ground cardamom
- ½ teaspoon paprika
- Salt

Directions:

1. At 350 degrees F/ 175 degrees C, preheat your air fryer.
2. Coat salmon fillets with paprika, olive oil, cardamom, paprika, and salt and place into the air fryer basket.
3. Cook salmon for almost 10-12 minutes. Turn halfway through.
4. Serve and enjoy.

Tuna Steak With Niçoise Salad

Servings: 4
Cooking Time: 15 Minutes

Ingredients:
- 1 pound tuna steak
- Sea salt, to taste
- Ground black pepper, to taste
- ½ teaspoon red pepper flakes, crushed
- ¼ teaspoon dried dill weed
- ½ teaspoon garlic paste
- 1-pound green beans, trimmed
- 2 handfuls baby spinach
- 2 handfuls iceberg lettuce, torn into pieces
- ½ red onion, sliced
- 1 cucumber, sliced
- 2 tablespoons lemon juice
- 1 tablespoon olive oil
- 1 teaspoon Dijon mustard
- 1 tablespoon balsamic vinegar
- 1 tablespoon roasted almonds, coarsely chopped
- 1 tablespoon fresh parsley, coarsely chopped

Directions:
1. Pat the tuna steak dry.
2. Combine the salt, black pepper, red pepper, dill, garlic paste and toss with the tuna steak well.
3. Spritz the coated tuna steak with a nonstick cooking spray.
4. Cook the tuna steak at 400 degrees F/ 205 degrees C for 10 minutes, flipping halfway through.
5. When the time is up, remove the tuna steak and add the green beans.
6. Spritz green beans with a nonstick cooking spray.
7. Cook at 400 degrees F/ 205 degrees C for 5 minutes, shaking once or twice for evenly cooking.
8. Cut your tuna into thin strips and transfer to a salad bowl; add in the green beans.
9. Add in the onion, cucumber, baby spinach and iceberg lettuce.
10. Whisk the lemon juice, olive oil, mustard and vinegar.
11. Dress the salad and garnish with roasted almonds and fresh parsley. Bon appétit!

Scallops And Spring Veggies

Servings: 4
Cooking Time: 7 To 10 Minutes

Ingredients:

- ½ pound asparagus, ends trimmed, cut into 2-inch pieces
- 1 cup sugar snap peas
- 1 pound sea scallops
- 1 tablespoon lemon juice
- 2 teaspoons olive oil
- ½ teaspoon dried thyme
- Pinch salt
- Freshly ground black pepper

Directions:

1. Place the asparagus and sugar snap peas in the air fryer basket. Cook for 2 to 3 minutes or until the vegetables are just starting to get tender.
2. Meanwhile, check the scallops for a small muscle attached to the side, and pull it off and discard.
3. In a medium bowl, toss the scallops with the lemon juice, olive oil, thyme, salt, and pepper. Place into the air fryer basket on top of the vegetables.
4. Steam for 5 to 7 minutes, tossing the basket once during cooking time, until the scallops are just firm when tested with your finger and are opaque in the center, and the vegetables are tender. Serve immediately.

Old Bay Tilapia Fillets

Servings: 2
Cooking Time: 7 Minutes

Ingredients:

- 2 tilapia fillets
- 1 teaspoon old bay seasoning
- ½ teaspoon butter
- ¼ teaspoon lemon pepper
- Black pepper
- Salt

Directions:

1. Grease its air fryer basket with cooking spray.
2. Place prepared fish fillets into the air fryer basket and season with lemon pepper, old bay seasoning, black pepper, and salt.
3. Spray fish fillets with cooking spray and cook at almost 400 degrees F/ 205 degrees C for 7 minutes.
4. Serve and enjoy.

Air Fried Mussels With Parsley

Servings: 5
Cooking Time: 12 Minutes

Ingredients:
- 1 ⅔ pound mussels
- 1 garlic clove
- 1 teaspoon oil
- Black pepper to taste
- Parsley Taste

Directions:
1. Clean and scrape the mold cover and remove the byssus.
2. Pour the oil, clean the mussels and the crushed garlic in the air fryer basket.
3. At 425 degrees F/ 220 degrees C, preheat your air fryer and air fry for 12 minutes.
4. Towards the end of cooking, add black pepper and chopped parsley.
5. Finally, distribute the mussel juice well at the bottom of the basket, stirring the basket.

Seasoned Breaded Shrimp

Servings: 4
Cooking Time: 15 Minutes

Ingredients:
- Olive oil
- 2 teaspoons Old Bay seasoning, divided
- ½ teaspoon garlic powder
- ½ teaspoon onion powder
- 1 pound large shrimp, deveined, with tails on
- 2 large eggs
- ½ cup whole-wheat panko bread crumbs

Directions:
1. Spray a fryer basket lightly with olive oil.
2. In a medium bowl, mix together 1 teaspoon of Old Bay seasoning, garlic powder, and onion powder. Add the shrimp and toss with the seasoning mix to lightly coat.
3. In a separate small bowl whisk the eggs with 1 teaspoon water.
4. In a shallow bowl, mix together the remaining 1 teaspoon Old Bay seasoning and the panko bread crumbs.
5. Dip each shrimp in the egg mixture and dredge in the bread crumb mixture to evenly coat.
6. Place the shrimp in the fryer basket, in a single layer. Lightly spray the shrimp with oil. You many need to cook the shrimp in batches.
7. Air fry until the shrimp is cooked through and crispy, 10 to 15 minutes, shaking the basket at 5-minute intervals to redistribute and evenly cook.

Crumbed Fish Fillets With Parmesan Cheese

Servings: 4
Cooking Time: 25 Minutes
Ingredients:
- 2 eggs, beaten
- ½-teaspoon tarragon
- 4 fish fillets, halved
- ½ tablespoon dry white wine
- ⅓ cup Parmesan cheese, grated
- 1 teaspoon seasoned salt
- ⅓-teaspoon mixed peppercorns
- ½-teaspoon fennel seed

Directions:
1. Add the Parmesan cheese, salt, peppercorns, fennel seeds, and tarragon to your food processor; blitz for about 20 seconds.
2. Drizzle dry white wine on the top of these fish fillets.
3. In a shallow dish, dump the egg.
4. Now, coat the fish fillets with the beaten egg on all sides, then coat them with the seasoned cracker mix.
5. Air-fry at 345 degrees F/ 175 degrees C for about 17 minutes. Bon appétit!

Homemade Lobster Tails Ever

Servings: 2
Cooking Time: 7 Minutes
Ingredients:
- 2 (6-ounce) lobster tails
- 1 teaspoon fresh cilantro, minced
- ½ teaspoon dried rosemary
- ½ teaspoon garlic, pressed
- 1 teaspoon deli mustard
- Sea salt, to taste
- Ground black pepper, to taste
- 1 teaspoon olive oil

Directions:
1. In addition to the lobster tails, combine the remaining ingredients well and coat the lobster tails well on all sides.
2. Cook the lobster tails at 370 degrees F/ 185 degrees C for 7 minutes, flipping halfway through.
3. Serve warm and enjoy!

Tuna Patties

Servings: 3 Servings
Cooking Time: 1 Hour 10 Minutes

Ingredients:
- 2 (7-oz.) cans of albacore tuna fish in the water (drained)
- 2 whisked eggs
- ½ cup of chopped onions
- ¼ cup of chopped fresh parsley
- 1 stack of celery
- ½ chopped red bell pepper
- 1 cup of panko crumbs
- ¼ cup + 3 tablespoons of grated Parmesan cheese
- 1 teaspoon of minced garlic
- 1 teaspoon of sriracha
- 1 tablespoon of lime juice
- 1 tablespoon of butter
- 1 tablespoon of olive oil
- ¼ teaspoon of salt
- ½ teaspoon of oregano
- Pinch of black pepper, to taste

Directions:
1. Add butter and oil in a skillet. Warm it on medium-high heat. Add in the bell pepper, garlic, and onions. Sauté for 5–7 minutes.
2. Drain the tuna cans and transfer them into a medium bowl. Squeeze it with lime juice.
3. Transfer the cooked vegetables into the bowl. Add in parsley, celery, oregano, sriracha, pepper, salt, half cup of panko crumbs, and 3 tablespoons of cheese. Mix it well.
4. Add in the whisked eggs, mix, and form 6 same-sized patties. If your patties are falling apart, add extra panko crumbs. Keep it in a refrigerator for 20–60 minutes.*
5. Mix in a separate bowl a half cup of panko crumbs with ¼ cup of grated cheese. Remove patties from the refrigerator and coat them with this mixture. Spray tops with some oil.
6. Preheat your air fryer to 390°F. Cover the inside of air fryer basket with the perforated parchment paper.
7. Put patties in the air fryer in a single layer. Avoid touching each other. Cook at 390°F for 4 minutes. Gently flip it, spray with oil, and cook for another 4 minutes.
8. Serve warm and enjoy your Tuna Patties!

Coconut Shrimp

Servings: 4
Cooking Time: 5 To 7 Minutes

Ingredients:

- 1 (8-ounce) can crushed pineapple
- ½ cup sour cream
- ¼ cup pineapple preserves
- 2 egg whites
- ⅔ cup cornstarch
- ⅔ cup sweetened coconut
- 1 cup panko bread crumbs
- 1 pound uncooked large shrimp, thawed if frozen, deveined and shelled
- Olive oil for misting

Directions:

1. Drain the crushed pineapple well, reserving the juice.
2. In a small bowl, combine the pineapple, sour cream, and preserves, and mix well. Set aside.
3. In a shallow bowl, beat the egg whites with 2 tablespoons of the reserved pineapple liquid. Place the cornstarch on a plate. Combine the coconut and bread crumbs on another plate.
4. Dip the shrimp into the cornstarch, shake it off, then dip into the egg white mixture and finally into the coconut mixture.
5. Place the shrimp in the air fryer basket and mist with oil. Air-fry for 5 to 7 minutes or until the shrimp are crisp and golden brown.
6. Did You Know? Shrimp are graded by how many there are in a pound. Large shrimp are usually 26 to 30 per pound, medium shrimp are 36 to 45 per pound. You can buy them shelled, deveined, and ready to cook, or fully cooked.

Red Snapper With Hot Chili Paste

Servings: 4
Cooking Time: 15 Minutes

Ingredients:

- 4 red snapper fillets, boneless
- A pinch of salt and black pepper
- 2 garlic cloves, minced
- 1 tablespoon coconut aminos
- 1 tablespoon lime juice
- 1 tablespoon hot chili paste
- 1 tablespoon olive oil

Directions:

1. In addition to the fish, mix up the other ingredients in a bowl and stir well.
2. Use the mixture to rub the fish, then place the fish in the basket of your air fryer.
3. Cook for 15 minutes at 380 degrees F/ 195 degrees C.
4. Serve with a side salad.

Southwestern Prawns With Asparagus

Servings: 3
Cooking Time: 5 Minutes

Ingredients:
- 1-pound prawns, deveined
- ½ pound asparagus spears, cut into 1-inch chinks
- 1 teaspoon butter, melted
- ¼ teaspoon oregano
- ½ teaspoon mixed peppercorns, crushed
- Salt, to taste
- 1 ripe avocado
- 1 lemon, sliced
- ½ cup chunky-style salsa

Directions:
1. Toss your prawns and asparagus with melted butter, oregano, salt and mixed peppercorns.
2. Cook the prawns and asparagus at 400 degrees F/ 205 degrees C for 5 minutes, shaking the air fryer basket halfway through the cooking time.
3. Divide the prawns and asparagus between serving plates and garnish with avocado and lemon slices. Serve with the salsa on the side. Bon appétit!

Asian Swordfish

Servings: 4
Cooking Time: 6 To 11 Minutes

Ingredients:
- 4 (4-ounce) swordfish steaks
- ½ teaspoon toasted sesame oil (see Tip)
- 1 jalapeño pepper, finely minced
- 2 garlic cloves, grated
- 1 tablespoon grated fresh ginger
- ½ teaspoon Chinese five-spice powder
- ⅛ teaspoon freshly ground black pepper
- 2 tablespoons freshly squeezed lemon juice

Directions:
1. Place the swordfish steaks on a work surface and drizzle with the sesame oil.
2. In a small bowl, mix the jalapeño, garlic, ginger, five-spice powder, pepper, and lemon juice. Rub this mixture into the fish and let it stand for 10 minutes.
3. Roast the swordfish in the air fryer for 6 to 11 minutes, or until the swordfish reaches an internal temperature of at least 140°F on a meat thermometer. Serve immediately.

Seafood Spring Rolls

Servings: 4
Cooking Time: 22 Minutes

Ingredients:
- Olive oil
- 2 teaspoon minced garlic
- 2 cups finely sliced cabbage
- 1 cup matchstick cut carrots
- 2 (4-ounce) cans tiny shrimp, drained
- 4 teaspoons soy sauce
- Salt
- Freshly ground black pepper
- 16 square spring roll wrappers

Directions:
1. Spray a fryer basket lightly with olive oil. Spray a medium sauté pan with olive oil.
2. Add the garlic to the sauté pan and cook over medium heat until fragrant, 30 to 45 seconds. Add the cabbage and carrots and sauté until the vegetables are slightly tender, about 5 minutes.
3. Add the shrimp and soy sauce and season with salt and pepper, then stir to combine. Sauté until the moisture has evaporated, 2 more minutes. Set aside to cool.
4. Place a spring roll wrapper on a work surface so it looks like a diamond. Place 1 tablespoon of the shrimp mixture on the lower end of the wrapper.
5. Roll the wrapper away from you halfway, then fold in the right and left sides, like an envelope. Continue to roll to the very end, using a little water to seal the edge. Repeat with the remaining wrappers and filling.
6. Place the spring rolls in the fryer basket in a single layer, leaving room between each roll. Lightly spray with olive oil. You may need to cook them in batches.
7. Air fry for 5 minutes. Turn the rolls over, lightly spray with olive oil, and cook until heated through and the rolls start to brown, 5 to 10 more minutes.

Crispy Fish Tacos

Servings: 5 Servings
Cooking Time: 40 Minutes

Ingredients:
- 1 pound of the firm and white fish
- 3 eggs
- 2 cups of sour cream
- ¾ cup of AP flour
- 1 package of corn tortillas
- 1 cup of panko bread crumbs
- 1–2 limes
- 1 teaspoon of cumin
- 1 teaspoon of onion powder
- 1 teaspoon of garlic powder
- 1 teaspoon of salt
- 1 teaspoon of black pepper
- 1 teaspoon of red chili flakes (optional)
- 1 teaspoon of lemon pepper (optional)
- Lettuce leaves, salsa, avocado, tomatoes, radishes, cabbage, and/or hot sauce, for serving

Directions:
1. Thaw the fish fillets and dry them with a paper towel. Cut into 2–3 pieces depending on the size of the fillets. Season both sides with pepper and salt.
2. Add AP flour in one bowl. Whisk 3 eggs in a separate bowl. Mix the panko bread crumbs, lemon pepper, cumin, red chili flakes, onion powder, garlic powder, ½ teaspoon of salt and pepper in a third bowl.
3. Dip the fish piece into the flour, then into the whisked eggs, and finally into the bread crumb mixture, lightly pressing it. Put the coated fillet on a big plate. Repeat this step with the remaining part of the fish.
4. Preheat your air fryer to 370ºF. Spray some oil inside the air fryer basket.
5. Transfer the coated fillets into the preheated basket; avoid them touching. Cook at 370ºF for 6 minutes. Gently flip it and cook for another 6 minutes. Remove and set aside. Repeat this step until all pieces of fish are cooked.
6. To cook the lime crema: Add the sour cream in a small bowl. Add in zest and juice from 2 limes. Season with a pinch of salt and whisk it with a fork.
7. To serve: Warm tortillas in a microwave or on the pan. Put the crispy fish in the middle. Top with the prepared lime crema and add vegetables or hot sauce you like.*
8. Serve warm and enjoy your Crispy Fish Tacos!

Vegetable Side Dishes Recipes
Radishes And Green Onions Mix

Servings: 4
Cooking Time: 15 Minutes
Ingredients:
- 20 radishes, halved
- 1 tablespoon olive oil
- 3 green onions, chopped
- Black pepper and salt to the taste
- 3 teaspoons black sesame seeds
- 2 tablespoons olive oil

Directions:
1. In a suitable bowl, mix all the recipe ingredients and toss well.
2. Put the radishes in your air fryer basket, Cook at almost 400 degrees F/ 205 degrees C for almost 15 minutes.
3. Serve.

Crispy Tofu With Soy Sauce

Servings: 4
Cooking Time: 35 Minutes
Ingredients:
- 1 block firm tofu, pressed and diced
- 1 tablespoon arrowroot flour
- 2 teaspoon sesame oil
- 1 teaspoon vinegar
- 2 tablespoon soy sauce

Directions:
1. In a suitable bowl, toss tofu with oil, vinegar, and soy sauce and let sit for almost 15 minutes.
2. Toss marinated tofu with arrowroot flour.
3. Grease its air fryer basket with cooking spray.
4. Add tofu in air fryer basket and cook for 20 minutes at 370 degrees F/ 185 degrees C. Shake basket halfway through.
5. Serve and enjoy.

Lush Summer Rolls

Servings: 4
Cooking Time: 15 Minutes

Ingredients:

- 1 cup shiitake mushroom, sliced thinly
- 1 celery stalk, chopped
- 1 medium carrot, shredded
- ½ teaspoon finely chopped ginger
- 1 teaspoon sugar
- 1 tablespoon soy sauce
- 1 teaspoon nutritional yeast
- 8 spring roll sheets
- 1 teaspoon corn starch
- 2 tablespoons water

Directions:

1. In a bowl, combine the ginger, soy sauce, nutritional yeast, carrots, celery, mushroom, and sugar.
2. Mix the cornstarch and water to create an adhesive for the spring rolls.
3. Scoop a tablespoonful of the vegetable mixture into the middle of the spring roll sheets. Brush the edges of the sheets with the cornstarch adhesive and enclose around the filling to make spring rolls.
4. Preheat the air fryer to 400°F (204°C). When warm, place the rolls inside and air fry for 15 minutes or until crisp.
5. Serve hot.

Sweet Potatoes With Tofu

Servings: 8
Cooking Time: 35 Minutes

Ingredients:

- 8 sweet potatoes, scrubbed
- 2 tablespoons olive oil
- 1 large onion, chopped
- 2 green chilies, deseeded and chopped
- 8 ounces (227 g) tofu, crumbled
- 2 tablespoons Cajun seasoning
- 1 cup chopped tomatoes
- 1 can kidney beans, drained and rinsed
- Salt and ground black pepper, to taste

Directions:

1. Preheat the air fryer to 400°F (204°C).
2. With a knife, pierce the skin of the sweet potatoes and air fry in the air fryer for 30 minutes or until soft.
3. Remove from the air fryer, halve each potato, and set to one side.
4. Over a medium heat, fry the onions and chilies in the olive oil in a skillet for 2 minutes until fragrant.
5. Add the tofu and Cajun seasoning and air fry for a further 3 minutes before incorporating the kidney beans and tomatoes. Sprinkle some salt and pepper as desire.
6. Top each sweet potato halve with a spoonful of the tofu mixture and serve.

Cheesy Roasted Tomatoes

Servings: 4
Cooking Time: 6 Minutes
Ingredients:
- Olive oil
- 4 Roma tomatoes, cut into ½ inch slices
- Salt
- ½ cup shredded mozzarella cheese
- ¼ cup shredded Parmesan cheese
- Freshly ground black pepper
- Parsley flakes

Directions:
1. Spray a fryer basket lightly with olive oil.
2. Season the tomato slices lightly with salt.
3. Place the tomato slices in the fryer basket in a single layer. You may need to cook these in batches.
4. Sprinkle each tomato slice with 1 teaspoon of mozzarella cheese. Sprinkle ½ teaspoon of shredded Parmesan cheese on top of the mozzarella cheese on each tomato slice.
5. Season with black pepper and sprinkle parsley flakes over the top of the cheeses.
6. Air fry until the cheese is melted, bubbly, and lightly browned, 5 to 6 minutes.

Simple Turmeric Cauliflower Rice

Servings: 4
Cooking Time: 20 Minutes
Ingredients:
- 1 big cauliflower, florets separated and riced
- 1 ½ cups chicken stock
- 1 tablespoon olive oil
- Salt and black pepper to the taste
- ½ teaspoon turmeric powder

Directions:
1. Combine together all the ingredients in a suitable pan.
2. Toss well.
3. Then cook in your air fryer at 360 degrees F/ 180 degrees C for 20 minutes.
4. When the cooking time is up, serve on plates as a side dish.

Simple Pesto Gnocchi

Servings: 4
Cooking Time: 15 Minutes

Ingredients:
- 1 (1-pound / 454-g) package gnocchi
- 1 medium onion, chopped
- 3 cloves garlic, minced
- 1 tablespoon extra-virgin olive oil
- 1 (8-ounce / 227-g) jar pesto
- ⅓ cup grated Parmesan cheese

Directions:
1. Preheat the air fryer to 340°F (171°C).
2. In a large bowl combine the onion, garlic, and gnocchi, and drizzle with the olive oil. Mix thoroughly.
3. Transfer the mixture to the air fryer and air fry for 15 minutes, stirring occasionally, making sure the gnocchi become light brown and crispy.
4. Add the pesto and Parmesan cheese, and give everything a good stir before serving.

Crispy Spiced Asparagus

Servings: 5
Cooking Time: 15 Minutes

Ingredients:
- ¼ cup almond flour
- ½ teaspoon garlic powder
- ½ teaspoon smoked paprika
- 10 medium asparagus, trimmed
- 2 large eggs, beaten
- 2 tablespoons parsley, chopped
- Salt and pepper to taste

Directions:
1. Before cooking, heat your air fryer to 350 degrees F/ 175 degrees C for about 5 minutes.
2. Combine garlic powder, smoked paprika, almond flour, and parsley in a mixing bowl.
3. To season, add salt and pepper.
4. Dredge the asparagus in the beaten eggs and then coat the asparagus with almond flour mixture.
5. Cook in your air fryer at 350 degrees F/ 175 degrees C for 15 minutes.

Spicy Sweet Potatoes

Servings: 4
Cooking Time: 15 Minutes
Ingredients:
- Olive oil
- 1½ teaspoon salt
- 1 teaspoon chili powder
- 1 teaspoon paprika
- 1 teaspoon onion powder
- ½ teaspoon ground cumin
- ½ teaspoon freshly ground black pepper
- ¼ teaspoon cayenne pepper
- 2 large sweet potatoes, peeled and cut into 1-inch pieces

Directions:
1. Spray a fryer basket lightly with olive oil.
2. In a small bowl, combine the salt, chili powder, paprika, onion powder, cumin, black pepper, and cayenne pepper.
3. In a large bowl, add the sweet potato and spray lightly with olive oil. Add the seasoning mix and toss to coat.
4. Put the sweet potatoes in the fryer basket. Air fry until browned and slightly crispy, about 15 minutes, shaking the basket every 5 minutes and spraying lightly with olive oil each time. To make them extra crispy, cook for a few more minutes but watch closely to make sure they don't burn.

Easy Rosemary Green Beans

Servings: 1
Cooking Time: 5 Minutes
Ingredients:
- 1 tablespoon butter, melted
- 2 tablespoons rosemary
- ½ teaspoon salt
- 3 cloves garlic, minced
- ¾ cup chopped green beans

Directions:
1. Preheat the air fryer to 390°F (199°C).
2. Combine the melted butter with the rosemary, salt, and minced garlic. Toss in the green beans, coating them well.
3. Air fry for 5 minutes.
4. Serve immediately.

Spiced Cauliflower Medley

Servings: 4
Cooking Time: 15 Minutes

Ingredients:
- 1 pound cauliflower florets, roughly grated
- 3 eggs, whisked
- 3 tablespoons butter, melted
- Salt and black pepper to the taste
- 1 tablespoon sweet paprika

Directions:
1. Set heat to high and then melt the butter in a pan.
2. Then add the cauliflower in the pan and cook until brown for 5 minutes.
3. Add salt, the whisked eggs, paprika, and pepper. Toss well.
4. Cook in your air fryer at 400 degrees F/ 205 degrees C for 10 minutes.
5. Serve on plates.

Roasted Bell Peppers With Garlic

Servings: 4
Cooking Time: 22 Minutes

Ingredients:
- 1 red bell pepper
- 1 yellow bell pepper
- 1 orange bell pepper
- 1 green bell pepper
- 2 tablespoons olive oil, divided
- ½ teaspoon dried marjoram
- Pinch salt
- Freshly ground black pepper
- 1 head garlic

Directions:
1. Slice the bell peppers into 1-inch strips.
2. In a large bowl, toss the bell peppers with 1 tablespoon of the oil. Sprinkle on the marjoram, salt, and pepper, and toss again.
3. Cut off the top of the garlic head and place the cloves on an oiled square of aluminum foil. Drizzle with the remaining olive oil. Wrap the garlic in the foil.
4. Place the wrapped garlic in the air fryer and roast for 15 minutes, then add the bell peppers. Roast for 7 minutes or until the peppers are tender and the garlic is soft. Transfer the peppers to a serving dish.
5. Remove the garlic from the air fryer and unwrap the foil. When cool enough to handle, squeeze the garlic cloves out of the papery skin and mix with the bell peppers.

Mushroom Risotto Croquettes

Servings: 4
Cooking Time: 15 Minutes

Ingredients:

- 2 garlic cloves, peeled and minced
- ½ cup mushrooms, chopped
- 6 ounces cooked rice
- 1 tablespoon rice bran oil
- 1 onion, chopped
- Sea salt as needed
- ¼ teaspoon ground black pepper
- 1 tablespoon Colby cheese, grated
- 1 egg, beaten
- 1 cup breadcrumbs
- ½ teaspoon dried dill weed
- 1 teaspoon paprika

Directions:

1. Add oil, onion, and garlic in a medium sized saucepan. Heat the pan over medium heat for a few minutes until turn soft.
2. Then add the mushrooms in the pan. Cook until the liquid thickens. Cool down the mixture.
3. Add and combine salt, black pepper, dill, paprika, and the cooked rice together.
4. Then mix with cheese. Divide the mixture into risotto balls.
5. Dip in the beaten eggs and coat the balls with breadcrumbs.
6. On a flat kitchen surface, plug your air fryer and turn it on.
7. At 390 degrees F/ 200 degrees C, heat your air fryer for 4 to 5 minutes in advance. Gently grease your air fryer basket with cooking oil or spray.
8. Arrange the balls evenly on the basket. Then cook in your air fryer for 7 minutes.
9. If needed, cook 2 more minutes.
10. When cooked, remove from the air fryer and serve warm with marinara sauce.

Roasted Brussels Sprouts

Servings: 4
Cooking Time: 20 Minutes

Ingredients:
- 1 pound fresh Brussels sprouts
- 1 tablespoon olive oil
- ½ teaspoon salt
- ⅛ teaspoon pepper
- ¼ cup grated Parmesan cheese

Directions:
1. Trim the bottoms from the Brussels sprouts and pull off any discolored leaves. Toss with the olive oil, salt, and pepper, and place in the air fryer basket.
2. Roast for 20 minutes, shaking the air fryer basket twice during cooking time, until the Brussels sprouts are dark golden brown and crisp.
3. Transfer the Brussels sprouts to a serving dish and toss with the Parmesan cheese. Serve immediately.
4. Did You Know? Brussels sprouts were cultivated in Roman times and introduced into the United States in the 1880s. Most Brussels sprouts in this country are grown in California.

Breadcrumb Crusted Agnolotti

Servings: 6
Cooking Time: 14 Minutes

Ingredients:
- 1 cup flour
- Black pepper and salt
- 4 eggs, beaten
- 2 cups breadcrumbs
- Cooking spray

Directions:
1. Mix flour with black pepper and salt.
2. Dip pasta into the flour, then into the egg, and finally in the breadcrumbs.
3. Spray with oil and arrange in the preheated air fryer in an even layer.
4. Set its temperature to 400 degrees F/ 205 degrees C and cook for 14 minutes, turning once halfway through cooking.
5. Cook until nice and golden.
6. Serve with goat cheese.

Roasted Corn On The Cob

Servings: 4
Cooking Time: 10 Minutes

Ingredients:
- 4 ears corn, shucked and halved crosswise
- 1 tablespoon extra-virgin olive oil
- Salt
- Pepper

Directions:
1. Place the corn in a large bowl. Coat with the olive oil and season with salt and pepper to taste.
2. Place the corn in the air fryer. Cook for 6 minutes.
3. Cool before serving.

Corn Pakodas

Servings: 5
Cooking Time: 8 Minutes

Ingredients:
- 1 cup flour
- ¼ teaspoon baking soda
- ¼ teaspoon salt
- ½ teaspoon curry powder
- ½ teaspoon red chili powder
- ¼ teaspoon turmeric powder
- ¼ cup water
- 10 cobs baby corn, blanched
- Cooking spray

Directions:
1. Preheat the air fryer to 425ºF (218ºC).
2. Cover the air fryer basket with aluminum foil and sprtiz with the cooking spray.
3. In a bowl, combine all the ingredients, save for the corn. Stir with a whisk until well combined.
4. Coat the corn in the batter and put inside the air fryer.
5. Air fry for 8 minutes until a golden brown color is achieved.
6. Serve hot.

Cheddar Tomatillos With Lettuce

Servings: 4
Cooking Time: 4 Minutes

Ingredients:
- 2 tomatillos
- ¼ cup coconut flour
- 2 eggs, beaten
- ¼ teaspoon ground nutmeg
- ¼ teaspoon chili flakes
- 1 ounce Cheddar cheese, shredded
- 4 lettuce leaves

Directions:
1. Cut the tomatillos into slices.
2. Mix ground nutmeg, chili flakes, and beaten eggs in a bowl.
3. Brush the tomatillo slices with the egg mixture. Then coat with coconut flour.
4. Repeat above steps with the rest slices.
5. Before cooking, heat your air fryer to 400 degrees F/ 205 degrees C.
6. Place the coated tomatillo slices in the air fryer basket in a single layer.
7. Cook in your air fryer for 2 minutes from each side.
8. When cooked, add the lettuce leaves on the top of the tomatillos.
9. To serve, sprinkle with shredded cheese.

Garlic Kale Mash

Servings: 4
Cooking Time: 20 Minutes

Ingredients:
- 1 cauliflower head, florets separated
- 4 teaspoons butter, melted
- 4 garlic cloves, minced
- 3 cups kale, chopped
- 2 scallions, chopped
- A pinch of black pepper and salt
- ⅓ cup coconut cream
- 1 tablespoon parsley, chopped

Directions:
1. In a pan that fits the air fryer, combine the cauliflower with the butter, garlic, scallions, salt, black pepper and the cream, toss, introduce the pan in the machine and cook at almost 380 degrees F/ 195 degrees C for 20 minutes.
2. Mash the mix well, add the remaining ingredients, whisk, divide between plates and serve.

Fried Pickles With Mayo Sauce

Servings: 2
Cooking Time: 10 Minutes

Ingredients:

- 1 egg, whisked
- 2 tablespoons buttermilk
- ½ cup fresh breadcrumbs
- ¼ cup Romano cheese, grated
- ½ teaspoon onion powder
- ½ teaspoon garlic powder
- 1 ½ cups dill pickle chips

- Mayo Sauce:
- ¼ cup mayonnaise
- ½ tablespoon mustard
- ½ teaspoon molasses
- 1 tablespoon ketchup
- ¼ teaspoon black pepper

Directions:

1. In a suitable shallow bowl, whisk the egg with buttermilk.
2. In another bowl, mix the breadcrumbs, cheese, onion powder, and garlic powder.
3. Dredge the pickle chips in the egg mixture, then, in the breadcrumb/cheese mixture.
4. Cook the mixture in the preheated air fryer at about 400 degrees F/ 205 degrees C for 5 minutes; shake the basket and cook for 5 minutes more.
5. Meanwhile, mix all the sauce ingredients until well combined. Serve the fried pickles with the mayo sauce for dipping.

Cheese Spinach

Servings: 6
Cooking Time: 16 Minutes

Ingredients:

- 1-pound fresh spinach
- 6 ounces gouda cheese, shredded
- 8 ounces cream cheese
- 1 teaspoon garlic powder
- 1 tablespoon onion, minced
- Black pepper
- Salt

Directions:

1. At 370 degrees F/ 185 degrees C, preheat your air fryer.
2. Grease its air fryer basket with cooking spray and set aside.
3. Spray a large pan with cooking spray and heat over medium heat.
4. Add spinach to the same pan and cook until wilted.
5. Add cream cheese, garlic powder, and onion and stir until cheese is melted.
6. Remove pan from heat and add Gouda cheese and season with black pepper and salt.
7. Transfer spinach mixture to the prepared baking dish and place into the air fryer.
8. Cook for 16 minutes.
9. Serve and enjoy.

Mushroom Mozzarella Risotto

Servings: 4
Cooking Time: 20 Minutes

Ingredients:
- 1-pound white mushrooms, sliced
- ¼ cup mozzarella, shredded
- 1 cauliflower head, florets separated and riced
- 1 cup chicken stock
- 1 tablespoon thyme, chopped
- 1 teaspoon Italian seasoning
- A pinch of salt and black pepper
- 2 tablespoons olive oil

Directions:
1. Grease a suitable baking pan with oil and then heat to medium heat.
2. Add the cauliflower rice and mushrooms. Toss and cook for a few minutes.
3. Add the shredded mozzarella, chicken stock, Italian seasoning, salt, and black pepper in the pan.
4. Cook in your air fryer at 360 degrees F/ 180 degrees C for 20 minutes.
5. To serve, sprinkle the chopped thyme on the top.

Desserts And Sweets
Almond Pecan Muffins

Servings: 12
Cooking Time: 15 Minutes

Ingredients:
- 4 eggs
- 1 teaspoon vanilla
- ¼ cup almond milk
- 2 tablespoons butter, melted
- ½ cup swerve
- 1 teaspoon psyllium husk
- 1 tablespoon baking powder
- ½ cup pecans, chopped
- ½ teaspoon ground cinnamon
- 2 teaspoons allspice
- 1 ½ cups almond flour

Directions:
1. Before cooking, heat your air fryer to 370 degrees F/ 185 degrees C.
2. In a bowl, beat the butter, sweetener, almond milk, whisked eggs, and vanilla together with a hand mixer until smooth.
3. Then mix all the remaining ingredients together until well combined.
4. Divide the batter into the silicone muffin molds.
5. Cook in batches in the preheated air fryer for 15 minutes.
6. Serve and enjoy!

Cinnamon Butter Muffins

Servings: 2
Cooking Time: 10 Minutes

Ingredients:

- 1 teaspoon of cocoa powder
- 2 tablespoons coconut flour
- 2 teaspoons swerve
- ½ teaspoon vanilla extract
- 2 teaspoons almond butter, melted
- ¼ teaspoon baking powder
- 1 teaspoon apple cider vinegar
- ¼ teaspoon ground cinnamon

Directions:

1. After adding the cocoa powder, coconut flour, swerve, vanilla extract, almond butter, baking powder, apple cider vinegar and ground cinnamon, use a spoon to stir them until smooth.
2. Pour the brownie mixture in the muffin molds and let them rest for 10 minutes.
3. Cook the muffins at 365 degrees F/ 185 degrees C for 10 minutes.
4. Cool them completely before serving.

Walnut Banana Split

Servings: 8
Cooking Time: 15 Minutes

Ingredients:

- 3 tablespoons coconut oil
- 1 cup panko breadcrumbs
- ½ cup of corn flour
- 2 eggs
- 4 bananas, peeled and halved lengthwise
- 3 tablespoons sugar
- ¼ teaspoon ground cinnamon
- 2 tablespoons walnuts, chopped

Directions:

1. In a suitable skillet, melt the coconut oil over medium heat and cook the breadcrumbs until they are golden brown and crumbly, for about 4 minutes. Stirconstantly.
2. Transfer the breadcrumbs to a shallow bowl and set aside to cool.
3. In a second bowl, place the cornmeal.
4. In a third bowl, beat the eggs.
5. Coat the banana slices with the flour, dip them in the eggs and finally coat them evenly with the breadcrumbs.
6. In a suitable bowl, mix the sugar and cinnamon.
7. Set the cook time to 10 minutes and set the temperature to 280 degrees F/ 140 degrees C on the air fryer.
8. Arrange banana slices in Air Fry Basket and sprinkle with cinnamon sugar.
9. Transfer banana slices to plates to cool slightly.
10. Sprinkle with chopped walnuts.

Vanilla Cobbler With Hazelnut

Servings: 4
Cooking Time: 30 Minutes

Ingredients:
- ¼ cup heavy cream
- 1 egg, beaten
- ½ cup almond flour
- 1 teaspoon vanilla extract
- 2 tablespoons butter, softened
- ¼ cup hazelnuts, chopped

Directions:
1. Mix up heavy cream, egg, almond flour, vanilla extract, and butter.
2. Then whisk the mixture gently. At 325 degrees F/ 160 degrees C, preheat your air fryer.
3. Layer its air fryer basket with baking paper.
4. Pour ½ part of the batter in the baking pan, flatten it gently and top with hazelnuts.
5. Then pour the remaining batter over the hazelnuts and place the pan in the air fryer.
6. Cook the cobbler for 30 minutes.

Honey Donuts

Servings: 8
Cooking Time: 8 Minutes

Ingredients:
- 1 cup coconut flour
- 4 eggs
- 4 tablespoons coconut oil, melted
- 1 teaspoon baking soda
- ⅔ cup apple cider vinegar:
- 1 teaspoon cinnamon
- 3 tablespoons honey
- a pinch of salt

Directions:
1. Let the air fryer pre-heat to 350 degrees F/ 175 degrees C.
2. Spray oil on a baking tray, spray a generous amount of grease with melted coconut oil.
3. In a suitable bowl, add apple cider vinegar, honey, melted coconut oil, salt mix well, then crack the 4 eggs, and mix it all together.
4. In another bowl, sift the coconut flour, baking soda, and cinnamon so that the dry ingredients will combine well.
5. Add the wet ingredients in a bowl and mix with the dry ingredients until completely combined.
6. Pour the prepared batter into the prepared donut baking pan. And add the batter into cavities.
7. Let it air fry for 10 minutes or 8 minutes at 350 degrees F/ 175 degrees C, or until light golden brown.
8. Serve right away and enjoy.

Creamy Cheesecake Bites

Servings: 16
Cooking Time: 2 Minutes
Ingredients:

- 8 ounces cream cheese, softened
- 2 tablespoons erythritol
- ½ cup almond flour
- ½ tsp vanilla
- 4 tablespoons heavy cream
- ½ cup erythritol

Directions:
1. In a stand mixer, mix cream cheese, 2 tbsp. heavy cream, vanilla, and ½ cup erythritol until smooth.
2. Line a plate with parchment paper and spread the cream cheese onto the parchment.
3. Refrigerate for 1 hour.
4. Mix together 2 tbsp. Erythritol and almond flour in a small bowl.
5. Drip the remaining heavy cream over the cheesecake bites and dip in the almond flour mixture to coat.
6. Arrange evenly the cheesecake bites inside the air fryer basket and cook in the air fryer at 350 degrees F/ 175 degrees C for 2 minutes.
7. Halfway cooking, check the cheesecake bites to ensure they are still frozen.
8. Serve with chocolate syrup on the top.

Vanilla Custard

Servings: 2
Cooking Time: 25 Minutes
Ingredients:

- 5 eggs
- 2 tablespoons swerve
- 1 teaspoon vanilla
- ½ cup unsweetened almond milk
- ½ cup cream cheese

Directions:
1. Add eggs in a suitable bowl and beat using a hand mixer.
2. Add cream cheese, sweetener, vanilla, and almond milk and beat for 2 minutes more.
3. Spray 2 ramekins with cooking spray.
4. Pour batter into the prepared ramekins.
5. At 350 degrees F/ 175 degrees C, preheat your Air fryer.
6. Place ramekins into the air fryer and cook for 20 minutes.
7. Serve and enjoy.

Grilled Curried Fruit

Servings: 8
Cooking Time: 5 Minutes

Ingredients:
- 2 peaches
- 2 firm pears
- 2 plums
- 2 tablespoons melted butter
- 1 tablespoon honey
- 2 to 3 teaspoons curry powder

Directions:
1. Cut the peaches in half, remove the pits, and cut each half in half again. Cut the pears in half, core them, and remove the stem. Cut each half in half again. Do the same with the plums.
2. Spread a large sheet of heavy-duty foil on your work surface. Arrange the fruit on the foil and drizzle with the butter and honey. Sprinkle with the curry powder.
3. Wrap the fruit in the foil, making sure to leave some air space in the packet.
4. Put the foil package in the basket and grill for 5 to 8 minutes, shaking the basket once during the cooking time, until the fruit is soft and tender.

Delicious Walnut Bars

Servings: 4
Cooking Time: 16 Minutes

Ingredients:
- 1 egg
- ⅓ cup cocoa powder 3 tablespoons swerve
- 7 tablespoons ghee, melted 1 teaspoon vanilla extract
- ¼ cup almond flour
- ¼ cup walnuts, chopped
- ½ teaspoon baking soda

Directions:
1. Thoroughly mix up all of the ingredients in a bowl.
2. Arrange the mixture to the cooking pan lined with parchment paper.
3. Cook at 330 degrees F/ 165 degrees C for 16 minutes.
4. Cool the bars before serving.

Low Carb Cheesecake Muffins

Servings: 18
Cooking Time: 30 Minutes

Ingredients:
- ½ cup Splenda
- 1 ½ cup cream cheese
- 2 eggs
- 1 teaspoon vanilla Extract

Directions:
1. At 300 degrees F/ 150 degrees C, preheat your air fryer.
2. Spray the muffin pan with oil.
3. In a suitable bowl, add the sugar alternative, vanilla extract, and cream cheese. Mix well.
4. Add in the eggs gently, 1 at a time. Do not over mix the batter.
5. Let it air fry for 25 to 30 minutes, or until cooked.
6. Serve.

Peanut Butter Banana Pastry Bites

Servings: 12
Cooking Time: 40 Minutes

Ingredients:
- 12 wonton wrappers
- 1 banana, cut into 12 pieces
- ½ cup peanut butter
- Cooking oil

Directions:
1. Lay out the wonton wrappers on a work surface. A clean table or large cutting board works well.
2. Place 1 banana slice and 1 teaspoon of peanut butter on each wrapper.
3. Fold each wrapper diagonally across to form a triangle. Bring the 2 bottom corners up toward each other. Do not close the wrapper yet. Bring up the 2 open sides and push out any air. Squeeze the open edges together to seal.
4. Spray the air fryer basket with cooking oil.
5. Place the bites in the air fryer basket and cook in batches, or stack (see Air fryer cooking tip). Spray with cooking oil. Cook for 10 minutes.
6. Remove the basket and flip each bite over.
7. Return the basket to the air fryer. Cook for an additional 5 to 8 minutes, until the bites have reached your desired level of golden brown and crisp.
8. If cooking in batches, remove the cooked bites from the air fryer, then repeat steps 5 through 7 for the remaining bites.
9. Cool before serving.

Erythritol Pineapple Slices

Servings: 4
Cooking Time: 20 Minutes
Ingredients:
- 4 pineapple slices
- 1 teaspoon cinnamon
- 2 tablespoons Erythritol

Directions:
1. Add pineapple slices, sweetener, and cinnamon into the zip-lock bag.
2. Shake well and keep in the refrigerator for 30 minutes.
3. At 350 degrees F/ 175 degrees C, preheat your air fryer.
4. Place pineapples slices into the air fryer basket and cook for 20 minutes.
5. Turn halfway through.
6. Serve and enjoy.

Honey-roasted Pears With Ricotta

Servings: 4
Cooking Time: 18 To 23 Minutes
Ingredients:
- 2 large Bosc pears, halved and seeded (see Tip)
- 3 tablespoons honey
- 1 tablespoon unsalted butter
- ½ teaspoon ground cinnamon
- ¼ cup walnuts, chopped
- ¼ cup part skim low-fat ricotta cheese, divided

Directions:
1. In a 6-by-2-inch pan, place the pears cut-side up.
2. In a small microwave-safe bowl, melt the honey, butter, and cinnamon. Brush this mixture over the cut sides of the pears.
3. Pour 3 tablespoons of water around the pears in the pan. Roast the pears for 18 to 23 minutes, or until tender when pierced with a fork and slightly crisp on the edges, basting once with the liquid in the pan.
4. Carefully remove the pears from the pan and place on a serving plate. Drizzle each with some liquid from the pan, sprinkle the walnuts on top, and serve with a spoonful of ricotta cheese.

Cauliflower Rice Plum Pudding

Servings: 4
Cooking Time: 25 Minutes

Ingredients:

- 1 ½ cups cauliflower rice
- 2 cups coconut milk
- 3 tablespoons stevia
- 2 tablespoons ghee, melted
- 4 plums, pitted and chopped

Directions:

1. In a suitable bowl, mix all the recipe ingredients, toss, divide into ramekins, put them in the air fryer, and cook at almost 340 degrees F/ 170 degrees C for 25 minutes.
2. Cool down and serve.

Apple Turnovers

Servings: 4 Servings
Cooking Time: 45 Minutes

Ingredients:

- 2 diced medium Granny Smith apples
- 6 tablespoons of brown sugar
- ¼ cup of powdered sugar
- ½ package pastry (14 ounces) for crust pie
- 4 tablespoons of butter
- 1 teaspoon of cornstarch
- 1 teaspoon of ground cinnamon
- 1 teaspoon of milk
- 2 teaspoons of cold water
- ½ tablespoon of oil

Directions:

1. Put the diced apples, cinnamon, brown sugar, and butter into a non-stick skillet. Cook on medium heat for 5 minutes until it softened.
2. Dissolve the cornstarch in cold water. Pour it into the apples and cook for 1 minute until it thickened. Remove it from the heat and allow to cool.
3. Spread some flour over the work surface, place the dough on it, and roll it out. Cut the rolled dough into rectangles small enough so that 2 can fit in the air fryer at a time. You should make 8 equal rectangles at the end.
4. Put some apple mixture in the center of the rectangles, about ½-inch from each edge. Roll out the other 4 rectangles to make them slightly larger than the filled ones. Put the larger rectangles on the top of the fillings and push the edges down with a fork to stick. Make small cuts in the center of the tops of the pies. Grease the tops with oil.
5. Preheat your air fryer to 385ºF. Grease the inside of the air fryer basket with some oil.
6. Place the prepared pies into the preheated air fryer basket. Cook at 385ºF for about 8 minutes until golden-brown. Remove them out and cook the other part of the pies.
7. Whisk milk with powdered sugar in a small bowl. Glaze the warm pies with the milk-sugar mixture.
8. Serve warm and enjoy your Apple Turnovers!

Chocolate Cake With Raspberries

Servings: 5-6
Cooking Time: 3 Minutes

Ingredients:
- 2 eggs
- ⅔ cup all-purpose flour
- 5 tablespoons sugar
- ⅔ cup unsalted butter
- Salt as needed
- 1 cup chocolate chips, melted
- ⅓ cup raspberries

Directions:
1. On a flat kitchen surface, plug your air fryer and turn it on.
2. Preheat your air fryer for about 4-5 minutes to 355 degrees F/ 180 degrees C. Gently grease 6 ramekins with oil and dust some sugar inside.
3. Whisk the butter and sugar in a medium sized bowl. Then beat the eggs in the mixture till fluffy.
4. Combine together with salt and flour. Then mix in the melted chocolate chips until well combined.
5. Then divide the mixture into the prepared ramekins with ¼ empty.
6. Transfer the ramekins onto the air fryer basket.
7. Cook the chocolate cake in the preheated air fryer for 3 minutes.
8. When cooked, remove from the air fryer.
9. Sprinkle the raspberries on the top and serve warm.

Cookies With Mashed Strawberry

Servings: 4
Cooking Time: 9 Minutes

Ingredients:
- 2 teaspoons butter, softened
- 1 tablespoon Splenda
- 1 egg yolk
- ½ cup almond flour
- 1 oz. strawberry, chopped, mashed

Directions:
1. In a suitable bowl, mix the butter, Splenda, egg yolk and almond flour well. Knead the non-sticky dough.
2. Form the small balls from the dough and use your finger to make small holes in each ball.
3. Fill the balls with the mashed strawberries.
4. Arrange to the balls to the cooking pan lined with baking paper and cook them at 360 degrees F/ 180 degrees C for 9 minutes.
5. When done, serve and enjoy.

Stuffed Apples

Servings: 4
Cooking Time: 12 To 17 Minutes

Ingredients:
- 4 medium apples, rinsed and patted dry (see Tip)
- 2 tablespoons freshly squeezed lemon juice
- ¼ cup golden raisins
- 3 tablespoons chopped walnuts
- 3 tablespoons dried cranberries
- 2 tablespoons packed brown sugar
- ⅓ cup apple cider

Directions:
1. Cut a strip of peel from the top of each apple and remove the core, being careful not to cut through the bottom of the apple. Sprinkle the cut parts of the apples with lemon juice and place in a 6-by-2-inch pan.
2. In a small bowl, stir together the raisins, walnuts, cranberries, and brown sugar. Stuff one-fourth of this mixture into each apple.
3. Pour the apple cider around the apples in the pan.
4. Bake in the air fryer for 12 to 17 minutes, or until the apples are tender when pierced with a fork. Serve immediately.

Enticing Ricotta Cheese Cake

Servings: 8
Cooking Time: 30 Minutes

Ingredients:
- 3 eggs, lightly beaten
- 1 teaspoon baking powder
- ½ cup ghee, melted
- 1 cup almond flour
- ⅓ cup erythritol
- 1 cup ricotta cheese, soft

Directions:
1. Combine the beaten eggs, baking powder, melted ghee, almond flour, erythritol, and soft ricotta cheese in a large mixing bowl.
2. Gently grease a baking dish that fits in your air fryer.
3. Add the mixture onto the prepared baking dish. Transfer the baking dish inside your air fryer.
4. Cook in the air fryer at 350 degrees F/ 175 degrees C for 30 minutes.
5. When cooked, remove from the air fryer and cool.
6. Then slice the cake into your desired size and serve.
7. Enjoy!

Zucchini Bars With Cream Cheese

Servings: 12
Cooking Time: 15 Minutes

Ingredients:
- 3 tablespoons coconut oil, melted 6 eggs
- 3 ounces' zucchini, shredded 2 teaspoons vanilla extract
- ½ teaspoon baking powder
- 4 ounces' cream cheese
- 2 tablespoons erythritol

Directions:
1. Whisk the coconut oil, zucchini, vanilla extract, baking powder, cream cheese, and erythritol in a bowl, then pour in the cooking pan lined with parchment paper.
2. Cook at 320 degrees F/ 160 degrees C for 15 minutes.
3. Slice and cool down.
4. Serve and enjoy.

Curry Peaches, Pears, And Plums

Servings: 8
Cooking Time: 5 Minutes

Ingredients:
- 2 peaches
- 2 firm pears
- 2 plums
- 2 tablespoons melted butter
- 1 tablespoon honey
- 2 to 3 teaspoons curry powder

Directions:
1. Preheat the air fryer to 325ºF (163ºC).
2. Cut the peaches in half, remove the pits, and cut each half in half again. Cut the pears in half, core them, and remove the stem. Cut each half in half again. Do the same with the plums.
3. Spread a large sheet of heavy-duty foil on the work surface. Arrange the fruit on the foil and drizzle with the butter and honey. Sprinkle with the curry powder.
4. Wrap the fruit in the foil, making sure to leave some air space in the packet.
5. Put the foil package in the basket and bake for 5 to 8 minutes, shaking the basket once during the cooking time, until the fruit is soft.
6. Serve immediately.

Dark Chocolate Soufflé

Servings: 6
Cooking Time: 15 Minutes

Ingredients:
- 3 eggs, separated
- 1 teaspoon vanilla
- ¼ cup swerve
- 5 tablespoons butter, melted
- 2 tablespoons heavy cream
- 2 tablespoons almond flour
- 2 oz. dark chocolate, melted

Directions:
1. Mix together melted chocolate and butter.
2. In a suitable bowl, whisk egg yolk with sweetener until combined.
3. Add almond flour, heavy cream, and vanilla and whisk well.
4. In a separate bowl, whisk egg white s until soft peaks form.
5. Slowly add the egg white to the chocolate mixture and fold well.
6. Pour chocolate mixture into the ramekins and place into the air fryer.
7. Cook at almost 330 degrees F/ 165 degrees C for 12 minutes.
8. Serve and enjoy.

Recipe Index

A

Air Fried Mussels With Parsley 61
Air-fried Chicken Wings And Waffles 17
Almond Pecan Muffins 79
Apple Turnovers 86
Avocado Buttered Flank Steak 45
Awesome Lemony Green Beans 27
Asian Swordfish 65

B

Bbq Pork Chops With Vegetables 48
Breadcrumb Crusted Agnolotti 75
Buffalo Chicken Wings 37
Barbecued Chicken Skewers 38
Beef Meatballs With Chives 27
Beef And Vegetable Cubes 49
Beef And Cheddar Burgers 44
Beer Corned Beef 50

C

Chicken Burgers With Parmesan Cheese 37
Chicken Manchurian 35
Chicken And Veggies Salad 38
Chicken Satay 36
Chicken Sausages 13
Cheddar Mushroom Taquitos 11
Cheddar Tomatillos With Lettuce 77
Cheesy Beef Meatballs 50
Cheesy Jalapeño Poppers 28
Cheesy Roasted Tomatoes 70
Cheese Ground Pork 48
Cheese Spinach 78
Chocolate Cake With Raspberries 87
Cinnamon Butter Muffins 80

Cinnamon French Toast 15
Citrus Pork Loin Roast 47
Classical French Frittata 14
Crispy Fish Tacos 67
Crispy Herbed Salmon 56
Crispy Tofu With Soy Sauce 68
Crispy Spiced Asparagus 71
Crispy Chicken Strips 40
Crumbed Fish Fillets With Parmesan Cheese 62
Creamy Broccoli Omelet 16
Creamy Cheesecake Bites 82
Curry Peaches, Pears, And Plums 89
Cajun Fish Tacos 57
Cauliflower Rice Plum Pudding 86
Corn Pakodas 76
Cookies With Mashed Strawberry 87
Coconut Granola With Almond 26
Coconut Shrimp 64

D

Dried Fruit Beignets 15
Dark Chocolate Soufflé 90
Delicious Walnut Bars 83
Egg-cilantro Cups 12

E

Enticing Pork Meatballs 32
Enticing Ricotta Cheese Cake 88
Erythritol Pineapple Slices 85
Easy Rosemary Green Beans 72
Easy Air Fried Salmon 56

F

Flavorful Scrambled Eggs With Chorizo 19
Fried Pickles With Mayo Sauce 78

Fried Olives 22

Feta Stuffed Peppers With Broccoli 18

G

Glazed Tender Pork Chops 51

Grilled Curried Fruit 83

Grit And Ham Fritters 12

Greek Chicken Kebabs 34

Garlic Kale Mash 77

Garlic Pork Roast 51

Garlic Soy Chicken Thighs 33

Garlicky Radish Chips 28

Garlicky Cucumber Chips 22

H

Healthy Salmon With Cardamom 58

Homemade Lobster Tails Ever 62

Home-made Potatoes With Paprika 18

Homemade Chicken Drumsticks 31

Honey Donuts 81

Honey-roasted Pears With Ricotta 85

Hot Egg Cups 14

I

Italian Egg Cups 17

J

Jerk Pork Butt Pieces 54

L

Lime Cajun Shrimp 58

Lush Summer Rolls 69

Lollipop Lamb Chops 53

Low Carb Cheesecake Muffins 84

Low-carb Cheese-stuffed Jalapeño Poppers 23

M

Mini Chicken Meatballs 30

Mushroom Mozzarella Risotto 79

Mushroom Risotto Croquettes 74

Mustard-crusted Fish Fillets 57

Marinated Chicken With Peppercorns 43

Mayo Turkey Breasts 42

Mouthwatering Chicken Wings 36

Mozzarella Arancini 29

O

Old Bay Tilapia Fillets 60

Old Bay Shrimp 55

P

Pretzels 19

Parmesan Ranch Risotto 21

Parmesan Spinach Muffins 20

Parmesan Sausage Meatballs 45

Parmesan Cauliflower Dip 31

Peanut Butter Banana Pastry Bites 84

Pesto Bruschetta 24

Pork Tenderloin With Apple Juice 52

Pork And Ginger Meatball Bowl 44

Q

Quick And Easy Blueberry Muffins 13

R

Radishes And Green Onions Mix 68

Ranch Kale Chips 26

Red Snapper With Hot Chili Paste 64

Roasted Brussels Sprouts 75

Roasted Bell Peppers With Garlic 73

Roasted Nut Mixture 25

Roasted Pork Tenderloin 53

Roasted Chicken And Vegetable Salad 43

Roasted Corn On The Cob 76

Rosemary Lamb Chops 54

S

Shrimp And Rice Frittata 21

Simple Pesto Gnocchi 71

Simple Turmeric Cauliflower Rice 70

Spinach And Artichoke Dip Wontons 23

Spicy Sweet Potatoes 72

Spice Chicken With Broccoli 41

Spiced Mixed Nuts 25

Spiced Cauliflower Medley 73

Stuffed Apples 88

Steak Fingers 49

Sweet Potatoes With Tofu 69

Sweet And Spicy Pork Chops 46

Sweet And Sour Chicken Drumsticks 35

Sweet-and-sour Drumsticks 40

Sweet-and-sour Polish Sausage 46

Sausage And Cream Cheese Biscuits 11

Seafood Spring Rolls 66

Seasoned Breaded Shrimp 61

Seasoned Chicken Thighs With Italian Herbs 39

Southwestern Prawns With Asparagus 65

Southern Fried Chicken 39

Scallops And Spring Veggies 60

T

Tuna Patties 63

Tuna Veggie Stir-fry 55

Tuna Steak With Niçoise Salad 59

Turkish Chicken Kebabs 34

Tasty Pasta Chicken 42

Tasty Shrimp Bacon Wraps 30

Teriyaki Chicken Bowls 41

Tomato Pork Burgers 47

Tortellini With Spicy Dipping Sauce 32

U

Unique Beef Cheeseburgers 52

V

Vanilla Custard 82

Vanilla Cobbler With Hazelnut 81

Veggie Shrimp Toast 29

Vegetable Quiche 20

W

Walnut Banana Split 80

Z

Zucchini Bars With Cream Cheese 89

Zucchini Fritters 16

Zucchini Chips With Cheese 24

Za'atar Chicken Thighs 33

Printed in Great Britain
by Amazon